amnesty international

KENYA

TORTURE, POLITICAL DETENTION AND UNFAIR TRIALS

Amnesty International is a worldwide movement independent of any government, political persuasion or religious creed. It plays a specific role in the international protection of human rights:

–it seeks the *release* of *prisoners of conscience.* These are people detained for their beliefs, colour, sex, ethnic origin, language or religion who have not used or advocated violence;

–it works for *fair and prompt trials* for all *political prisoners* and on behalf of political prisoners detained without charge or trial;

–it opposes the *death penalty* and *torture* or other cruel, inhuman or degrading treatment or punishment of *all prisoners* without reservation.

Amnesty International is impartial. It does not support or oppose any government or political system, nor does it support or oppose the views of the prisoners whose rights it seeks to protect. It is concerned solely with the protection of the human rights involved in each case, regardless of the ideology of the government or the beliefs of the victim.

Amnesty International, as a matter of principle, condemns the torture and execution of prisoners by anyone, including opposition groups. Governments have the responsibility for dealing with such abuses, acting in conformity with international standards for the protection of human rights.

Amnesty International does not grade governments according to their record on human rights: instead of attempting comparisons it concentrates on trying to end the specific violations of human rights in each case.

Amnesty International has an active worldwide membership, open to anyone who supports its goals. Through its network of members and supporters Amnesty International takes up individual cases, mobilizes public opinion and seeks improved international standards for the protection of prisoners.

Amnesty International acts on the basis of the United Nations Universal Declaration of Human Rights and other international instruments. Through practical work for prisoners within its mandate, Amnesty International participates in the wider promotion and protection of human rights in the civil, political, economic, social and cultural spheres.

Amnesty International has more than 500,000 members, subscribers and supporters in over 150 countries and territories, with over 3,400 local groups in more than 55 countries in Africa, the Americas, Asia, Europe and the Middle East. Each group works on behalf of at least two prisoners of conscience in countries other than its own. These countries are balanced geographically and politically to ensure impartiality. Information about prisoners and human rights violations emanates from Amnesty International's Research Department in London. No section, group or member is expected to provide information on their own country, and no section, group or member has any responsibility for action taken or statements issued by the international organization concerning their own country.

Amnesty International has formal relations with the United Nations (ECOSOC), UNESCO, the Council of Europe, the Organization of American States and the Organization of African Unity.

KENYA

TORTURE, POLITICAL DETENTION AND UNFAIR TRIALS

AI Index: AFR/32/17/87
ISBN: 0 86210 128 X
First published July 1987
Amnesty International Publications
1 Easton Street
London WC1X 8DJ
United Kingdom

SUDAN

ETHIOPIA

LAKE RUDOLF

UGANDA

Wajir

K E N Y A

SOMALIA

Kisumu

Nakuru

LAKE VICTORIA

Kisii

Naivasha

NAIROBI

Hola (Galole)

TANZANIA

Manyani

Mombasa

INDIAN OCEAN

T A B L E   O F   C O N T E N T S

APPENDICES

CENTRAL NAIROBI

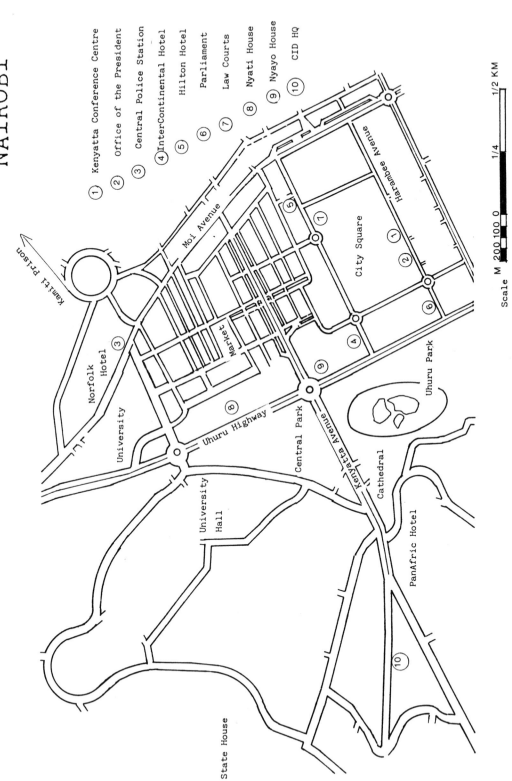

1. Kenyatta Conference Centre
2. Office of the President
3. Central Police Station
4. InterContinental Hotel
5. Hilton Hotel
6. Parliament
7. Law Courts
8. Nyati House
9. Nyayo House
10. CID HQ

Kamiti Prison

Norfolk Hotel

University

Moi Avenue

Market

Uhuru Highway

University Hall

Central Park

Kenyatta Avenue

Harambee Avenue

City Square

Cathedral

Uhuru Park

State House

PanAfric Hotel

Scale M 200 100 0   1/4   1/2 KM

KENYA: TORTURE, POLITICAL DETENTION AND UNFAIR TRIALS

1. INTRODUCTION

Amnesty International is concerned about numerous reports of torture of people arrested for suspected political opposition to the Kenyan Government, at least two of whom have died in custody. Ten people whom Amnesty International regards as prisoners of conscience have been detained without charge or trial for an indefinite period under administrative detention orders made on the grounds of public security. Over 75 other alleged political opponents have been imprisoned after unfair trials. Many of them may also be prisoners of conscience.

Those arrested on political grounds "disappeared" for days or even months while held incommunicado for interrogation by the police Special Branch. During this period they were held illegally without either being brought to court and charged with an offence or being detained under an official administrative detention order. The legal remedy for unlawful detention was ineffective as those responsible for law and justice failed to inquire into the cases and lawyers and families of the "disappeared" were often frightened into silence. In addition to the 10 untried detainees and over 75 convicted political prisoners mentioned above, several hundred other suspected political opponents have also been arrested and held for prolonged periods in unacknowledged and unlawful custody, when many were probably tortured or ill-treated before being eventually released without charge.

In the past year Amnesty International has made numerous appeals to the Government of Kenya about these abuses of human rights. In particular, the organization has urged the authorities to account for prisoners who "disappeared" after their arrest and has appealed for an official inquiry into allegations that prisoners have been tortured. It has called for the release of any people imprisoned solely for their non-violent opinions. The Kenyan authorities have not replied.

In December 1986 an Amnesty International delegate, Professor David Weissbrodt, visited Kenya to investigate the trials of political prisoners. He discussed the organization's concerns with the Attorney General and observed two political trials (see Appendix I). The Attorney General denied that prisoners had been held unlawfully or refused legal representation and he rejected the allegations that torture had been used.

Amnesty International subsequently wrote to President Daniel arap Moi on 30 January 1987 appealing for an urgent, impartial investigation into allegations of torture and for the introduction of further safeguards against torture, including an end to prolonged unlawful incommunicado detention of political prisoners. Amnesty International criticised the use of administrative detention under Public Security Regulations made under the Preservation of Public Security Act which provides for detention for an indefinite period without charge or trial "for the preservation of public security." Amnesty International also called for the release of anyone imprisoned solely for their non-violent opinions.

No reply has been received but in February 1987 President Moi, speaking to students at the University of Nairobi, said that Amnesty International should "leave Kenya alone" and that Kenya "needed no interference from Amnesty International "(The Nation, Nairobi, 26 February 1987).

Neither on that occasion nor in any subsequent public statement has any government official responded in detail to the criticisms which Amnesty International has made of human rights violations in Kenya. A " clean-up" of the police force was announced by the President on 4 April 1987, but Amnesty International's recommendations regarding torture, indefinite administrative detention without trial , "disappearances" and unlawful detention, unfair trials and other concerns have not been implemented by the authorities.

In view of the government's failure to respond to Amnesty International's appeals or to implement its recommendations, and considering the seriousness of the continuing violations of human rights, Amnesty International is publishing its conclusions in order to alert the international community to the situation and in the hope that the Kenyan Government will respond by taking steps to end these abuses and establish safeguards for the protection of human rights in the future.

2. BACKGROUND TO POLITICAL ARRESTS IN 1986-87

Kenya attained independence from the United Kingdom on 12 December 1963, under a government formed by Jomo Kenyatta, leader of the Kenya African National Union (KANU). A year later Kenya became a Republic under the Presidency of Jomo Kenyatta, who retained the position until his death in 1978. Amnesty International was concerned about a number of human rights issues under President Kenyatta's government, including the detention without trial of political opponents, several of whom were adopted by the organization as prisoners of conscience; the "disappearance" and murder in 1975 of J M Kariuki, a prominent government critic who was a member of parliament; allegations of torture and harsh treatment of political prisoners; and the death penalty.

President Kenyatta was succeeded in 1978 by the former Vice-President, Daniel arap Moi. All 26 political detainees held under President Kenyatta's government were freed by President Moi soon after his inauguration. They included four members of parliament - Jean-Marie Seroney, the former Deputy Speaker, George Anyona, Martin Shikuku, and Wasonga Sijeyo who had been held since 1969, when the opposition Kenya People's Union (KPU) which he represented in parliament, was banned and its leaders arrested; the writer, Ngugi wa Thiong'o; and a politician and journalist, Koigi wa Wamwere. All had been adopted by Amnesty International as prisoners of conscience. For the first four years of President Moi's government, there were no political detainees but in May 1982, George Anyona was detained again after announcing the imminent formation of an opposition party. The following month the government introduced a bill which changed the Constitution and made Kenya a one-party state. This bill also prohibited the formation of any political party other than the ruling KANU. Parliament passed the bill unanimously.

Other government critics were detained in June 1982 during increasing expressions of dissent, including the distribution of anti-government pamphlets called "Pambana", "Struggle" in Kiswahili, published by a clandestine organization, the December Twelfth Movement. The detainees adopted by Amnesty International as prisoners of conscience and held without charge or trial until 1983 and 1984 included John Khaminwa, a lawyer detained for representing a political detainee and challenging the validity of his detention, Mukaru Ng'ang'a and four other university lecturers. Maina wa Kinyatti, a university lecturer convicted of possessing a seditious document and sentenced to six years imprisonment, is still in prison and has been adopted by Amnesty International as a prisoner of conscience.

On 1 August 1982 there was a coup attempt by Kenya Air Force personnel in which many people were killed. Over 1,000 airforce personnel were arrested and later convicted by courts martial of treason, mutiny or other offences. Twelve were condemned to death and were executed in July 1985, including three men returned to Kenya by the Tanzanian authorities despite their having been granted asylum in Tanzania. Over 60 university students were arrested following demonstrations in favour of the coup attempt, and although the majority were released and pardoned by the President in early

Maina wa Kinyatti
jailed in 1982 for six years

Raila Odinga, detained
without trial since 1982

1983, 10 were jailed for sedition, four of whom are still serving sentences
of between five and 10 years' imprisonment. Four other men were arrested
after the coup attempt and were subsequently adopted by Amnesty
International as prisoners of conscience. Koigi Wamwere, a member of
parliament (who was not alleged to have been involved in the coup attempt)
was detained without explanation under the Public Security Regulations
until 1984. Otieno Mak'Onyango, a prominent journalist, Vincent Otieno, a
university professor, and Raila Odinga (son of ex-Vice-President Oginga
Odinga, the former leader of the KPU, who was himself held under house
arrest for some months) were initially charged with treason but the charges
were later dropped and they were detained without charge or trial under
Public Security Regulations. Otieno Mak'Onyango was released in December
1986, Vincent Otieno was released in 1983, but Raila Odinga remains in
prison. He has been adopted by Amnesty International as a prisoner of
conscience.

Amnesty International had also been concerned about the killings by
the security forces of several hundred people and the torture of numerous
others, all of Somali ethnic origin, in Wajir in north eastern Kenya in
February 1984; the imprisonment for several months and reported torture or
ill-treatment of some 19 university students arrested after demonstrations
in February 1985, in which at least one student and possibly several more
were killed; and the use of the death penalty - some 200 people are
reported to be under sentence of death for robbery with violence or murder.

In March 1986, a new wave of arrests of suspected government
opponents began. Those detained included Ngotho Kariuki, former Dean of
Commerce of Nairobi University; Kariuki Gathitu and Joseph Kamonye Manje,

both university lecturers, and Oyangi Mbaja, a business colleague of Oginga Odinga, a leading opposition figure. They were each held for over two weeks without official acknowledgement and, apparently, in breach of the law. A habeas corpus application was brought on behalf of Ngotho Kariuki: this resulted in an announcement that he had been detained indefinitely under the Public Security Regulations. Two of the others were brought to trial. Oyangi Mbaja was sentenced to 30 month's imprisonment after pleading guilty to a charge in court of "neglecting to report a felony" (namely the existence of an anti-government organization publishing seditious publications). Joseph Kamonye Manje was convicted of "possession of a seditious publication", and was imprisoned for five years. Kariuki Gathitu was served with an indefinite detention order issued under Public Security Regulations.

Other arrests of lecturers, students, journalists, businessmen, civil servants, teachers and farmers took place throughout 1986 until, by the end of the year, 10 people had been formally detained under Public Security Regulations and 50 had been convicted of political offences related to alleged links with Mwakenya, a clandestine socialist opposition organization. Between January and June 1987, at least 25 others were convicted of these or other political offences. Hundreds more are believed to have been arrested in similar circumstances for suspected political opposition and detained without legal basis for days or even weeks before being released without charge.

Detailed information about Mwakenya is not available to Amnesty International. Mwakenya is an acronym for Muungano wa Wazalendo wa Kukuomboa Kenya (Union of Nationalists for the Liberation of Kenya). The organization is secret and has no spokesmen or identified leaders. It has published and distributed numerous pamphlets, such as "Mpatanishi" ("The Unifier"), "Mzalendo" ("The Nationalist") and other documents describing its manifesto and reports of its meetings. It is said to be built on a cell-system, with oaths taken by members not to divulge their activities. Its members are believed to be recruited all over the country and to comprise people from many different ethnic groups.

Mwakenya advocates socialism in Kenya and has vigorously criticized the present government and political-economic system, both of which it seeks to overthrow. It draws on ideas associated with the anti-colonialist Mau-Mau rebellion in the 1950s. An issue of "Mzalendo" in April 1986 declared that Mwakenya had moved to guerrilla warfare. However, only one incident of any such armed activity has been reported: three former university students were convicted in July 1986 of sabotaging a railway line in order to derail a goods train. Amnesty International is concerned about certain aspects of their trials: they were held incommunicado and illegally for some weeks after arrest; two had broken limbs for which no satisfactory explanation was given in court; and they had no legal counsel. However, their admissions of guilt were accompanied by forthright statements in court criticizing the government and defending their actions, which they said were carried out "under the instructions of their Mwakenya commanders" (The Nation, Nairobi, 5 July 1986). They have not been adopted as prisoners of conscience by Amnesty International.

Precise details of Mwakenya's objectives and activities, such as when it was formed, its size, or its relation with any other clandestine political opposition group, such as the December Twelfth Movement, are not known to Amnesty International. Although a number of people who have been brought to court and tried since March 1986 have admitted being members of Mwakenya, Amnesty International considers that their admissions may not be fully reliable evidence in all cases, either in so far as they contain information about Mwakenya or with respect to their own involvement with it, because many appear to have made admissions under duress. Some of those sentenced for alleged involvement with Mwakenya may, in fact, be prisoners of conscience who have not in any way used or advocated violence against the government but who were threatened or tortured to the point where they "confessed" to acts which they had not committed. However, in nearly every case, Amnesty International has insufficient information about the opinions and activities of the individual prisoners before their arrest to know whether they were actively involved with Mwakenya and its advocacy of violence against the government or were simply peaceful critics of the government.

3. UNLAWFUL CUSTODY AND "DISAPPEARANCES"

Kenyan law stipulates that anyone who is arrested must be brought before a court or released within 24 hours. However, for over a year the authorities have repeatedly ignored this requirement. Prisoners have "disappeared" for several days and in some cases weeks after arrest. Over 75 prisoners who have pleaded guilty to political offences and all of the 10 prisoners who have been detained before 1986 and June 1987 under Public Security Regulations have been subjected to prolonged periods of unacknowledged and incommunicado detention by the Special Branch. During that time they effectively "disappeared". This is not only a flagrant breach of the law: it is in precisely these circumstances that torture is most likely to occur.

The period of such unlawful detention has varied between a week and three months. Peter Gathoga Kihara, for example, was allegedly held secretly for about three months before being brought to court in March 1986. Israel Otieno Agina was held incommunicado and without acknowledgement for over three months before being formally detained under the Public Security Regulations in December 1986. A large number of other people - possibly several hundreds - were arrested on suspicion of political opposition but were later released uncharged. Among them were two members of parliament, Charles Rubia and Abuya Abuya; Salim Lone, a journalist and United Nations' employee in New York, USA, arrested while visiting Kenya in July 1986 and later stripped of his Kenyan citizenship; and the wives of two prisoners of conscience - Mumbi wa Maina, the wife of Maina wa Kinyatti, and Ida Odinga, the wife of Raila Odinga. They were later released but all were held beyond the legal 24-hour limit and at least one of them is suing the government for unlawful detention and ill-treatment.

Sections 32, 33, 35 and 36 of the Criminal Procedure Code provide that an arrested person shall be released or brought before a magistrate within 24 hours from the time of the arrest, and if that is not possible, that the police should bring him or her before a magistrate "without unnecessary delay".

Article 72 (3) of the Constitution of Kenya also stipulates: "Any person who is arrested or detained ... and who is not released, shall be brought before a court as soon as is reasonably practicable, and where he is not brought before a court within twenty-four hours of his arrest or from the commencement of his detention, the burden of proving that the person arrested or detained has been brought before a court as soon as is reasonably practicable shall rest upon any person alleging that the provisions of this subsection have been complied with." This provision has also been ignored. In no case known to Amnesty International involving people arrested on political grounds have the authorities sought to justify the legality of the detention of such people, or been required by the courts to bring evidence in support of the legality of the detention.

The picture that emerges, then, is of wholesale disregard for the rights of prisoners and the requirements of the law by those empowered to uphold it, who have repeatedly resorted to practices which are both unlawful and unconstitutional in their pursuit of suspected opponents of the government. Moreover, their actions have been in direct violation of the provisions of the International Covenant on Civil and Political Rights (ICCPR), to which the Government of Kenya acceded in 1972. This treaty concerns rights contained in the Universal Declaration of Human Rights, and is binding on State Parties. Article 9 of the Covenant states: "Anyone arrested or detained on a criminal charge shall be brought promptly before a judge or other officer authorized by law to exercise judicial power and shall be entitled to trial within a reasonable time or to release....". The Human Rights Committee set up under the terms of this Covenant has stated in its general comment on Article 9 that delays in bringing a person before a judge or other officer "must not exceed a few days".

During the period of unlawful detention, the authorities in nearly all the cases would not acknowledge that the person was in custody, although they did not deny it. The prisoners had, in effect, "disappeared". After being arrested, by police officers in most cases, prisoners were initially taken to police stations. In some cases, the prisoners' names were not entered into the official record of prisoners held (the Occurrence Book) or were entered incorrectly, and prisoners were moved rapidly between different police stations, also apparently to conceal their whereabouts. Subsequently, most prisoners were transferred to the custody of the Special Branch.

The Special Branch is a special police unit responsible for internal security but apparently under the control of the Office of the President and not the Commissioner of Police. Most prisoners, irrespective of where they were arrested, were reportedly taken for interrogation to the Nairobi Province headquarters of the Special Branch in Nyayo House, a prestigious office block in central Nairobi near the Intercontinental Hotel.

Relatives and friends tried to trace the "disappeared" prisoners by searching for them at police stations, and the offices of the Police Criminal Investigation Department (CID) and the Special Branch, but without success. They were unable to obtain any information from the authorities. In a number of cases, the Commissioner of Police publicly stated that he knew nothing of the arrest. No reply could be obtained from the Special Branch.

Prisoners were transferred from Special Branch custody either to be released (after being threatened with reprisals if they spoke of their imprisonment) or to be moved to a civil prison (such as Kamiti maximum security prison in Nairobi) following a decision to detain them under Public Security Regulations, or to be taken to the police CID headquarters prior to being taken to court to be charged and tried. Hundreds of prisoners are believed to have been held secretly and incommunicado by the Special Branch for varying periods since March 1986 or even earlier, before being released.

When prisoners were brought to trial or when habeas corpus applications were made on their behalf, their unlawful detention, "disappearance" or secret and unacknowledged detention, and incommunicado detention, were not mentioned once by the magistrate or judge even though the date of arrest was officially noted in the court and the length of time since arrest could be calculated quite simply. The same magistrate, Chief Magistrate H H Buch, presided over most of the trials - which makes this omission the more astonishing. The Attorney General denied to Amnesty International's delegate in December 1986 that he knew of any instances of illegal detention. In November he had stated in parliament that people arrested should by law be brought to court within 24 hours or released, and that detention beyond this period was illegal and a criminal offence (Kenya Times, Nairobi, 14 November 1986).

Torture and ill-treatment of prisoners was facilitated by their "disappearance". They were held outside the protection of the law and without any relative, legal representative or doctor being allowed to see them. The allegations of torture by some of those held in these circumstances have been so consistent that Amnesty International has concluded that many, if not all, the detainees were tortured, ill-treated or threatened with torture, by the Special Branch during the period of their "disappearance".

The legal remedy for unlawful detention - a habeas corpus application - has proved to be ineffective. When Ngotho Kariuki "disappeared", a habeas corpus application resulted in a court ordering on 18 March 1986, 13 days after his arrest, that the police produce him in court on 21 March and explain why he should not be released. On that date however, the State Attorney disclosed in court that Ngotho Kariuki had been detained under Public Security Regulations on 17 March and that the state was consequently not obliged to produce him in court.

A habeas corpus application by the wife of Mirugi Kariuki, a lawyer arrested on 9 December 1986, led to a court order on 17 December that he be produced in court on 23 December and that the authorities explain why he should not be released. In court on that date the State Attorney disclosed that he had been detained under the Preservation of Public Security Act on 18 December, the day after the habeas corpus order, and he was not produced in court.

Gibson Kamau Kuria, a lawyer and law lecturer, who had submitted the habeas corpus application on behalf of Mirugi Kariuki, was himself the subject of a habeas corpus application when he "disappeared" after being arrested on 26 February 1987. When the application came to court on 12 March, the same State Attorney, Bernard Chunga, the Assistant Deputy Public Prosecutor, produced a detention order issued under Public Security Regulations on 6 March, eight days after his arrest. In none of these cases did the judge comment on the illegality of the prisoner's custody prior to the issuance of a detention order. In other cases where prisoners have "disappeared", habeas corpus applications were reported to have been abandoned when a detention order was imposed. No prisoner who has been the subject of a habeas corpus application has subsequently appeared in court.

Furthermore, it has become a common belief in Kenya that if a habeas corpus application is made, it will only result in the prisoner's official detention under Public Security Regulations; hence lawyers have been very reluctant to make such applications. In one case reported to Amnesty International, the family of a "disappeared" prisoner delayed making the habeas corpus application in the hope that he might be released, until reports that he was being tortured persuaded them to apply for habeas corpus. He was then detained under Public Security Regulations, but at least this meant he was transferred to a civil and no longer tortured.

So despite the legal and constitutional safeguards and remedies against unlawful detention and "disappearance" of prisoners, there is an established pattern of the Kenyan authorities denying that these abuses occur, either professing ignorance of them or refusing to comment about them.

Amnesty International has made numerous urgent appeals to the authorities - including the President, the Minister of State in the Office of the President responsible for internal security, the Attorney General, the Chief Justice, the Police Commissioner and the Director of the Special Branch - to clarify prisoners' legal status and whereabouts and to ensure that prisoners are either brought to court in accordance with the law or otherwise released. Amnesty International has not received a single reply to these appeals. The neglect and undermining of these crucial legal and constitutional safeguards of human rights, which appear to have been condoned by senior government officials and law officers, constitute a serious abuse of the rule of law.

4. TORTURE AND ILL-TREATMENT OF POLITICAL PRISONERS

Torture is prohibited by Article 74 (1) of the Constitution of Kenya which states that "No person shall be subject to torture or to inhuman or degrading punishment or other treatment". Nevertheless Amnesty International has received numerous reports that people arrested on political grounds are tortured, particularly those suspected of involvement with Mwakenya. These reports include first-hand testimony given to Amnesty International, statements by defendants in court, court documents, and information on the deaths of two prisoners who are believed to have been tortured.

In many cases full details of the allegations are not yet available because those able to give such testimony - such as prisoners, prisoners' families or released prisoners - fear reprisals. Many of those released from custody after torture were reportedly forced to sign a statement undertaking not to disclose any information about their imprisonment, under threat of rearrest and further torture.

Reports of the methods of torture used by the Special Branch - immersion in water, starvation, and beatings - are also consistent with allegations made by some political prisoners in the past. It is also significant that although a number of complaints of torture have been made in court against the police or Special Branch in recent years, hardly any of these complaints have been accepted by the courts. Although only a few cases of torture are described in detail below, Amnesty International believes that they are typical of an established pattern of torture of people arrested for political reasons.

The torture appears to be used primarily to obtain a confession of involvement in anti-government activities, particularly of links with Mwakenya. Those who did not respond to questions with a voluntary admission, or who made an admission when threatened with torture that they had committed an offence, have testified that they were tortured to confess to political offences which they claimed thay had not committed and to plead guilty in court. If they did not, they were threatened with further torture or indefinite detention under Public Security Regulations. Many reportedly preferred the outcome of a specific prison sentence, even of four or five years, to indefinite detention without trial, where conditions would be harsher. Prisoners' written "confessions" or other statements have not, in fact, been presented at their trials, where no other evidence was produced by the prosecution beyond their own admissions of guilt. Their guilty pleas and admissions were, however, in each case believed to be both the basis of the prosecution case against them and the basis for arresting and interrogating other people.

Many are believed to have agreed to plead guilty in court and admit the accusations against them because they were tortured or threatened with torture. Defendants were reportedly told by their interrogators that they should not complain in court about being illegally detained, denied access to lawyers or relatives or tortured or otherwise coerced into pleading guilty. They were also required to agree with the prosecution's summary of the case against them. In court, however, they were allowed to make pleas in mitigation on grounds of their family responsibilities, ill-health or repentance in order to obtain a less severe sentence than otherwise might be the case.

Defendants also appear to have felt coerced into agreeing to plead guilty by the presence of some of their interrogators in court - an indirect threat to the defendant not to change the plea. Prisoners who agreed to plead guilty were transferred from Special Branch custody to the CID headquarters, where a special unit was reportedly responsible for dealing with their cases. They were taken to court as quickly as possible. They had no access to legal counsel before or at their trial, their trials were held with virtually no public announcement and at unusual times, and their families were not informed of their trial and generally did not know what had happened to them since their arrest and "disappearance". In court, the trial began immediately, and was normally concluded within about half an hour.

Three defendants initially pleaded not guilty in court. In March 1986, Charles Kangara Njoroge, a businessman, was released by the judge when the prosecution withdrew the charge. He was rearrested outside the courtroom and "disappeared" again into custody. Six days later he reappeared in court and pleaded guilty to the same charge - he made no complaint and the Chief Magistrate did not inquire into these circumstances when convicting and imprisoning him. In April 1987, Peter Nyangau Momanyi pleaded not guilty to communicating political information to the Libyan embassy in Nairobi. The magistrate adjourned the case and remanded him back into custody. A week later he appeared in court again, still without a lawyer, pleaded guilty, and was sentenced to 15 months' imprisonment. A third defendant who pleaded not guilty to the same charge in April 1987 and also asked to see a lawyer was remanded in custody until July. Amnesty International believes that Charles Njoroge and Peter Momanyi may have both changed their pleas as a result of torture or other duress.

Some defendants attempted to contest the prosecution's summary of their case, or to complain of torture, ill-treatment, denial of medical treatment or threats, at the stage of trial following conviction when defendants could make pleas of mitigation. These complaints were all dismissed by the presiding magistrates. In cases of medical complaints the magistrates specified that medical treatment should be provided, but in no case did they order an inquiry into allegations of torture or ill-treatment.

Most victims of torture have reported that they were tortured by officers of the Special Branch, which is said to have a special unit for arresting, detaining and interrogating political prisoners.

The reports received by Amnesty International indicate that most detainees were tortured at Nyayo House, the Nairobi Province headquarters of the Special Branch, on Posta Road near the Intercontinental Hotel in Nairobi. There have also been reports of prisoners being tortured in Nyati House, the national headquarters of the Special Branch, near the University and Uhuru Highway, and at the CID headquarters on Milimani Road in Nairobi, opposite the Haran Court Hotel. Political prisoners held in police stations

Nyayo House, central Nairobi (tall building, centre), contains Special Branch interrogation centre

immediately after arrest were not usually reported to have been tortured there, although torture or ill-treatment of suspected criminals by the police is said to be frequent.

Amnesty International has not received reports of political prisoners being tortured once they have been transferred to an official prison under the Kenya Prison Service administration, such as Kamiti prison in Kamiti, northeast Nairobi. The exception to this was a report Amnesty International received in 1985 that students imprisoned on political grounds in Kamiti prison in Nairobi had been tortured by Special Branch officers.

The principle method of torture is nicknamed "the swimming pool". Prisoners in Nyayo House have been kept for up to five or seven days naked in a basement cell whose cement floor was flooded to a depth of about two inches. Victims have described being periodically sprayed with cold water from a hosepipe. They were denied any food while undergoing this torture. Some prisoners were allowed out of the cell to the toilet or to drink water from a tap, but others had to urinate or defecate in their flooded cell. Some prisoners reportedly developed bronchitis or pneumonia as a result of being kept wet and cold - at 2,600 metres above sea level, Nairobi experiences particularly cold temperatures at certain times of year. Prisoners also developed infections in open wounds and severe blistering of the skin. Nervous breakdowns and hallucinations were also reported. At least one prisoner required psychiatric treatment after being released.

The second method of torture described by many former prisoners usually occurred after they had been subjected to the water-torture for several days. They were taken for further interrogation, during which they were stripped and systematically beaten on the joints and various parts of the body in a way that left no lasting traces of torture. They were beaten with sticks, truncheons, chair-legs and pieces of rubber. They were also forced to do strenuous physical exercises, and beaten if they failed to do so. Prisoners were verbally humiliated and abused.

When not being kept in water or interrogated, prisoners were held in cells without furniture, whose walls were painted black with varied black and white paint on the ceiling and floor. A dim light was permanently on. These conditions contributed to the prisoners' general state of anxiety and tension.

In February 1987 notices to sue the government for illegal detention and torture were submitted to the courts by the lawyers of three administrative detainees and another detainee who died in custody. The following is the complaint of Mukaru Ng'ang'a, a former history lecturer who was arrested in April 1986:

"He was falsely imprisoned by Police Officers who were interrogating him, and was within the meaning of secion 74 (1) of the Kenya Constitution tortured unlawfully, punished and subjected to degrading and/or inhuman treatment and punishments in that he was humiliated by being forced to live for long periods alone from 5.4.86 to 4.7.86 (5 April 1986 to 4 July 1986) naked in a dark cell with water; was forced to wear his wet clothes when going to the interrogation chamber; was called by the interrogators a smelling, stinking rat and a smelling stinking professor; used to be kept for four to seven days in the cell with water without food or water whilst being prepared for the next session of interrogation and torture. In the course of interrogation outside the cell with water he was beaten with pieces of wood and tyres, rulers, by over 8 officers on all parts of his body including buttocks, ankles, joints and legs; was intimidated, threatened with being locked up in police cells for 5 years and death, detention or being tortured until he became a cripple unless he agreed to confess to a false charge in which event he would be released; suffered the agony of seeing his soles wearing off and his feet smelling as it had been stated prophetically; being threatened that a detention order in respect of him would be prepared but he would be held under torture until he confessed to false charges."

The complaint of Mirugi Kariuki, a lawyer arrested in December 1986, states:

"He was tortured unlawfully, punished and subjected to degrading and/or inhuman treatment and punishment in that he was not given any food from 10.12.86 until 20.12.86 (10 to 20 December 1986); he was savagely beaten all over his body many times by more than eleven police interrogators; one officer stepped on his testicles as he lay down, thereby causing very great pain to him; these officers used whips and pieces of timber and tyres; the beating resulted in wounds which were not treated until he was detained (ie formally issued with a detention order under Public Security Regulations, on 22 December 1986); his request for medical treatment was refused; he was kept naked in a cell with water from 11.12.86 to 20.12.86 (11 to 20 December 1986); he was sprayed with water coming out of a hose pipe at very

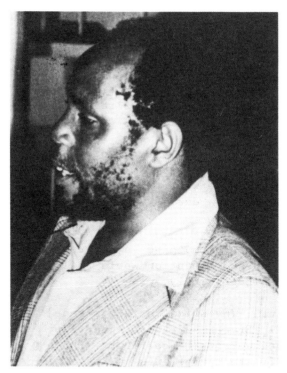

Mukaru Ng'ang'a, detained
indefinitely without trial

Mirugi Kariuki, detained
indefinitely without trial

great pressure thereby causing intense pain to him; he was humiliated, jeered at and bullied; he was denied an opportunity to sleep during that period; he suffers from attacks of asthma and during that period suffered four attacks; his requests that he be given drugs and that he be not kept in cold water were refused; he collapsed on 12.12.86 (12 December 1986) and his request for medical attention was refused; between 11.12.86 and 15.12.86 (11 to 15 December 1986) he was passing blood together with his urine and when he requested for medical care it was refused; even today he has problems with passing urine."

The lawyer who submitted these notices, Gibson Kamau Kuria, was himself arrested on 26 February 1987, shortly after they had been filed. Amnesty International believes that this was the main reason for his own arrest and subsequent detention under Public Security Regulations on 6 March 1987. In May, his legal partner, Kiraitu Mirungi, completed filing the four suits, for which a hearing date had yet to be set at the time of writing, early June 1987. The two other suits included complaints that Wanyiri Kihoro, a lawyer detained under Public Security Regulations in October 1986, had been tortured and illegally detained, and that Stephen Wanjema, a carpenter who died in custody in September 1986 had been illegally detained and tortured and that no inquest had been held into his death (see Chapter 5).

Some political prisoners also alleged that they had been tortured in their appeals against conviction to the High Court. The basis of the appeals was that since the defendants had pleaded guilty under duress their guilty pleas should be declared inadmissible and their convictions quashed.

In his appeal to the High Court against conviction in August 1986 for "neglecting to report a felony", Karige Kihoro, a businessman, stated:

"I was put in a waterlogged cell for periods of 60 hours and was continually beaten and was dictated statements alleging that I knew that some people intended to form an illegal party. I was forced to sign them as a condition of being removed from the water and having no alternative and being in pain I signed them.

"On 5th August 1986 I was told bluntly that I had only two choices of either pleading guilty to the charge of neglecting to report a felony or going to detention. I was forced to make a choice between two evils and I finally opted to plead guilty to the charge under duress and through coercion.

"It was made absolutely clear to me that if I changed my mind in court and pleaded not guilty the charge would be withdrawn and detention would follow forthwith. I did not want to rot in detention indefinitely.

"I was taken to court by C.I.D. (Criminal Investigation Department) officers in the company of several Special Branch officers who kept threatening me and hovering around me menacingly in the corridors of the court reminding me to plead guilty otherwise if the charge was withdrawn, the torture I would face would make the first one only a joke. When the charge was read to me I pleaded guilty in fear but when the particulars of the charge were read to me I was asked to say whether they were true or not. I said that some were true and the others were untrue. The trial magistrate did not ask me what was true or untrue, which was the proper thing for him to do at this stage. I believe this failure to seek my elaboration has occasioned me great injustice and that is precisely why I am in jail."

He also added that he had been denied legal representation between his arrest and trial and had been held incommunicado. His appeal against his sentence of 18 months' imprisonment was rejected on the grounds that he had pleaded guilty and had not complained of torture at his trial.

In his High Court appeal, John Gupta Ng'ang'a Thiong'o, a student, stated that the police had extracted a plea of guilt from him through "duress, coercion, inducement, undue influence, intimidation and trickery" during the seven days of his pre-trial detention. He had pleaded guilty "out of desperation and so as to avoid further acts of cruelty and police intimidation". The affidavit presented at his appeal by his lawyer stated:

"He was arrested on 8.5.86 (8 May 1986) at around 2pm near the Kenya School of Law, as he was leaving the school after lunch, and he was booked in at Kileleshwa Police Station (in Nairobi). At around 6pm, some police officers in plainclothes came to the station and blindfolded him. He was led to a motor vehicle in which he was told to lie down. The motor vehicle drove away for a very long distance and when it stopped he was taken to some place, while he was still blindfolded. When the blindfold was removed, he found himself in a dark underground cell in a place unknown to him. He remained there until 14.5.86 (14 May 1986).

John Gupta Ng'ang'a Thiong'o
jailed for 15 months

Karige Kihoro
jailed for 18 months

"On several occasions he was blindfolded and taken to a panel of interrogators who asked him many questions, then he was blindfolded again and returned to the underground cell. Throughout his incarceration in the dark underground cell he was not allowed any contact with the outside world and he felt isolated, abandoned and at the mercy of his captors. His captors kept telling him that they could do whatever they liked with him, and even if they killed him, nobody would ever know or do anything about it. When he told them that he would like to see a lawyer, they told him that there was no need for him to see one because if he did not plead guilty he would be detained.

"On 14.5.86 (14 May 1986) he was blindfolded and taken to a police station, where he was informed of the charges against him. A police officer at the station told him that he would not entertain any nonsense from him, and that if he did not plead guilty he would be detained straightaway. On 15.5.86 (15 May 1986) as he was being led to court by two police officers (they) repeated the threats to him and warned him in the court corridors that if he did not plead guilty to the charge they would withdraw the case, like they had done in Kangara's case and take him back to the cells until he pleaded guilty like Kangara had done [see p12]. He pleaded guilty because he did not want to be detained or returned to the dark underground cell. The only reason why this evidence was not adduced before the court... is that he was not a free agent at that time because the lengthy incommunicado incarceration in the underground cell had driven him to hopelessness and despair, and that, even in court he was still under the intimidation and undue influence of the police interrogators."

His appeal was dismissed on 6 February 1987 on the grounds that he had pleaded guilty in the lower court and had not submitted any complaint at the time.

Although press reports of Mwakenya-related trials have been brief, some have indicated that the defendants were tortured or ill-treated. Several defendants are reported to have complained of ill-treatment when they made mitigatory statements in the later part of their trials. However, the presiding magistrates did not inquire into the allegations in order to establish whether or not the guilty plea or admission of guilt made earlier in the trial might have been obtained under duress.

For example, Stephen Ngoroge Wanguthi, a civil servant sentenced to six years' imprisonment on 26 June 1986 for alleged distribution of a seditious publication, said in court that "while being interrogated by police he had gone through a rough time and was praying that the court should order that he be examined medically as he had developed nose bleeding and stomach problems". Instead of considering whether this information was relevant in assessing whether or not Stephen Wanguthi had pleaded guilty voluntarily, the Chief Magistrate simply ordered that the prisoner should be given medical treatment (The Nation, Nairobi 27 June 1986).

Other defendants complained in court of medical problems but did not indicate whether or not these were caused or exacerbated by ill-treatment in custody before trial.

TESTIMONIES OF TORTURE

Testimony "A"

This former prisoner has asked that his name should not be made public for fear of reprisals. He was arrested at his home in Nairobi in mid-1986. Three plainclothes officers entered the house at 3 am while one other person remained in their car. The three officers said they were members of the Special Branch. The officers searched the house for three hours and took away over 60 books, mostly socialist literature. No publications regarded as "seditious" in Kenya were found.

He was taken to a nearby police station. Although the police knew his name, they entered another name in the Occurrence Book. He was held alone in his cell until evening, when he was placed in the back of a Land Rover, blindfolded, and driven for 45 minutes. When the blindfold was removed, he found himself in a basement corridor with two rows of six cells on each side.

There was no furniture in the cell, which was about seven feet in length, seven feet in width, and 10 feet high. The cell had no window - two dim electric lights were left on most of the time. He slept on the floor with only a blanket and wore the same clothes throughout. There was a common toilet and sink which prisoners were allowed to use.

Occasionally he was blindfolded, taken to an elevator, and interrogated in a room high up in the same building. Interrogation sessions were irregular, sometimes twice a day and sometimes only once a week. At the first interrogation there were nine interrogators present, but usually there were two, four, or six questioners. The interrogators stated that they knew that he was a member of Mwakenya and questioned him on his membership.

Three days after his arrest, he was told to take off his clothes. The guards sprayed him with a high pressure water hose until the cell floor was covered with about one and a half inches of water. He was kept for five days in the water-filled cell. The guards came around from time to time to spray him with the hose and replenish the water level. During the five days he was kept in the water, he was given no food but he was permitted to go to the toilet or drink water from the sink. He was unable to sleep for the first two or three days in the water but eventually managed to sleep in a sitting position. He was not interrogated for the five days he stayed in the water. His feet hurt, and his skin swelled up.

He heard two other prisoners undergoing the water torture constantly coughing. One prisoner remained only a single night in the water before he began begging to talk to the interrogators. Other prisoners complained vocally of sores on their bodies, a broken leg, and a broken hand.

After he had spent five days in the water, the guards came back and placed him in another cell where he had first to sweep the water out. He was given food twice a day. His skin peeled after drying out and became very painful. The following week he was interrogated a second time but he refused to admit to being a member of Mwakenya.

He was subjected to the water torture for a second five-day period and interrogated again on other occasions.

After about six weeks in custody, he was taken again to the interrogation room and told to take off his clothing and do exercises - 50 or 60 situps, feet raisers, and putting the index finger on the floor while being forced to run in circles around the finger. When he got tired or he lifted his feet in an exposed position or as the opportunity arose, the interrogators abused him and hit him with stools and chair legs on his wrists, buttocks and ankles. The blows did not break the skin or cause lasting bruising. He was constantly verbally abused.

After about an hour of this, he was returned to his cell but was beaten in the same way the next day, for about the same period. During interrogation he was frequently threatened with administrative detention under the Public Security Regulations. He knew that such a detention order meant that he would be detained indefinitely for years without any hope of release. He was told that the food for those who were detainees was worse than what he was receiving and that no medical care was available for them.

Finally, the chief interrogator went to his cell and pressed him to plead guilty to the offence of "neglecting to report a felony", for which he would receive a light sentence of about one and a half year's imprisonment. At the same time he threatened him with detention under Public Security Regulations if he did not plead guilty. He refused to plead guilty, stating that he would prefer a detention order as he had committed no offence. The next day the chief interrogator returned to his cell and told him that they had been thinking about his case and had decided he could go home. Later, guards came to his cell, blindfolded him as usual, and took him up to the interrogation room. He was told that he would be permitted to go home that day but that he must sign a statement that his interrogation was not completed and that he would not reveal to anyone the nature of his interrogation. He signed the statement. He was taken back to his cell and was permitted to take a shower. He was then taken out blindfolded and put in the back of a Land Rover. He was driven around for about 10 minutes and then the vehicle stopped, his blindfold was removed and he was told to get out. He found himself in Moi Avenue and made his way home.

During the entire time of his interrogation, his wife had not known of his whereabouts. She had gone to the police and they said they did not know where he was. He later learned that he had been held in Nyayo House, the Nairobi Province headquarters of the Special Branch.

Testimony "B"

This prisoner was arrested in July 1986 and was taken to Special Branch custody in Nyayo House in Nairobi. In the following testimony he describes his arrest and torture:

"I arrived on Sunday morning at about 9am after spending the night at a police station. I had been kept there alone in a cell. I was driven here in a police Land Rover, which was terrifying as I did not know what the whole thing was about. The vehicle came to a stop, I heard a huge iron door open and the Land Rover moved in. The door was closed. The rear door of the vehicle was opened and I was ordered out. I was held by the hand by one or two people and moved into a building and then into a single room opening into a corridor. Somebody struck me on the back. The blindfold was not removed.

"I found the single room was about six feet by six feet in measurement. The ceiling walls were painted black and the floor had patches of white paint on black. The lights were in two thick fluorescent bulbs which were recessed into the upper part of the wall about seven feet up and protected by a metal grill. There was very little light in the cell.

"The following Wednesday afternoon, matters turned for the worse and I was told that I was being hostile. I was ordered to strip and was beaten mainly on the lower parts of legs below the knees. This lasted for 15 to 20 minutes. I was told I was going to be put in the "swimming pool". I pleaded I did not know how to swim. I was abused and told all manner of things. I was called a systematic liar. Another said, "We tame shrews here" - according to him, shrews are untamable creatures. When I was taken back to the basement I was ordered to remove all my clothes and then put in one of the cells. I was hosepiped with water until the room was about two inches deep flooded with water. The door was shut. I stayed there without food for three days.

"Every morning an officer passed by and asked if I had anything more to add to my story. The guards might allow you to go out to go to the toilet, otherwise you were supposed to do this in the cell. Every morning when the officer passed by from the first day to the end, I always said I had spoken the truth and had no more to add.

"On Friday afternoon I was ordered out and taken back to the seventh floor for further interrogation, then returned to the cell, which had been swept dry of water.

"On Sunday of the second week I was told to undress again and put back in the same room with water. I was hosepiped and left there to rot. I stayed in total isolation without food until Friday, when I started to hallucinate from starvation, I was taken back to the seventh floor and questioned further. When they made no progress, the order was given to hypnotise me. This was an awful experience..."

(The testimony continues with a passage referring to hallucinatory-type experiences derived from the prisoner's past, as well as his interrogation experience. This is extremely difficult to interpret and a medical expert who studied this passage for Amnesty International was unable to conclude whether any part of it represented an actual experience as distinct from a series of hallucinations caused by torture and hunger. Whether or not these hallucinations were generated by hypnosis, drugs, sensory deprivation or any other "trigger" could not be determined.)

In all, this prisoner underwent the "water torture" four times. He gave the following account of his fourth period of water torture:

"This is the fourth time in 55 days that I have been put in ankle-deep water, without clothes and food, around the clock, in a six foot by six foot cell and left to wear out and die. My feet have taken in too much water and are painful to walk on. It is as if a person is driving red hot pins through at times.

"During the first week here I was put in for three days. At the beginning of the second week, they put me in from Sunday to Saturday and hypnotised me so that I could tell them all. In their language, so that I can start "talking". Then for one week of the fifth week and now for a whole week. To be put in, you only need one official to say that you should be put in the "swimming pool". In all I have stayed 24 days in water. The whole experience is very painful. On the first week I got very, very hungry and started hallucinating. You sit with your bottom under water until it pains - the same goes for the legs - six days and seven nights with or without sleep...

"Since I was arrested, I was interrogated 18 times. Some of the sessions were over six hours long. I was beaten up once and was kept without clothes, without food, in isolation in ankle-deep water for a total of 24 days. Three of the water torture sessions were each one week long and the fourth session was three days long. I was hypnotised once and up to this day I still feel the after-effects of this in the form of "echoes in the brain". My legs have had sores since I was put in the water a second time. I told the authorities this but they appeared to delight in it - that their torture is having the desired effect on me. Nothing was done. I have had some problems with my stomach - ulcers, I think."

5. DEATHS IN CUSTODY

At least three people have died in custody in the past year, apparently as a result of torture. Two of them were suspected of involvement with Mwakenya. Peter Njenga Karanja, a prominent businessman from Nakuru, who was well-known as one of the few African rally drivers participating in the East African Safari rally, was arrested on 7 February 1987 in Nakuru. He subsequently "disappeared" and his family were unable to obtain any information on where he was held. Amnesty International's appeals to the authorities to explain his whereabouts and legal status brought no response. In early March his wife learnt that he had died at Kenyatta National Hospital in Nairobi on 28 February 1987 while still in custody. He had reportedly been tortured by members of the Special Branch in Nyayo House in Nairobi before being transferred to the hospital.

After some delay, the authorities arranged for a post-mortem examination at which his family's medical representative was present. The inquest into his death is due to be held in July 1987. The Minister of State responsible for internal security, Mr Justus ole Tipis, said in parliament that Peter Karanja had died of "pneumonia and gangrene of the intestine" and denied that his death was the result of torture (The Nation, 26 March 1987). An independent post-mortem report, however, also diagnosed dehydration, laceration of the membrane supporting the small intestine, and wounds and bruises on the limbs. The body was described as "emaciated" with the skin "peeling off in most of surface and in others there are blisters". Peter Karanja was described by his family as being "in good health" at the time of his arrest.

Stephen Wanjema, a carpenter, was arrested in Elburgon in western Kenya on 29 August 1986. He was also suspected of links with Mwakenya. He died in custody in Nakuru on 11 September. He is said to have been taken to hospital for treatment of injuries sustained in custody but to have been returned to prison from Nakuru hospital on 4 September. His family has filed a suit against the government alleging that he had been unlawfully detained and tortured, and that no inquest had been held into his death in custody.

Another prisoner who died after being tortured in police custody was Gregory Byaruhanga, a Ugandan teacher from Kisii in western Kenya. He was arrested in Kisii on 13 March 1987 and charged with illegal possession of foreign (Ugandan) currency and residing in Kenya illegally. Thousands of non-Kenyans were taken into custody around this time during mass arrests of suspected illegal aliens. Gregory Byaruhanga was held by the CID. He was taken to court on 20 March and remanded in Kisii prison. However, on 23 March, he was taken to hospital for urgent medical treatment and died the same day, still in police custody. A post-mortem was carried out the next day in the presence of the Ugandan diplomatic representative to Kenya.

The independent post-mortem diagnosis revealed "septicaemia following multiple linear septic wounds on the trunk and legs" as the cause of death. The final comment of the post-mortem stated: "The history from the medical records and from Dr...(the Kisii District Hospital Surgeon) shows that the

Peter Njenga Karanja
died in custody

Gregory Byaruhanga
died in custody

late Byaruhanga was assaulted and sustained widespread soft tissue injury and deep wounds that became septic probably because of neglect and delayed medical attention and this led to septicaemia and multiple organ failure - the liver, the lungs and the adrenals". An inquest is due to be held, although no date had been set at the time of writing. However, a police inspector from Kisii has been charged with the murder of Gregory Byaruhanga.

Gregory Byaruhanga's case differs from that those of Peter Karanja and Stephen Wanjema in that he was not accused of of any political offence such as having links with Mwakenya. However it illustrates other reports Amnesty International has received, indicating that police often ill-treat or torture criminal suspects and that prisoners are frequently not given necessary medical treatment.

There have been reports that at least four people have been killed in the last year, possibly by suicide after jumping, or after falling from a top floor in Nyayo House but Amnesty International has not been able to establish their identities or whether they had been held by the Special Branch.

Amnesty International has received other reports of people arrested on political grounds becoming seriously ill as a result of torture and having been released on medical grounds. Kiboi Kariuki, a former chairman of the Kenya Railways Union, who "disappeared" after being arrested on 22 October 1986, was only released at the end of December by the Special Branch who held him illegally without charge. He was reportedly released only because he was seriously ill and it was feared that he might die in custody unless he had urgent medical treatment.

6. POLITICAL TRIALS

Since March 1986 there have been over 75 trials of people accused of political offences, many of them in connection with Mwakenya. Amnesty International is concerned by a number of irregularities in the trial proceedings and believes that defendants were denied the right to a fair trial in accordance with international legal standards.

The defendants were neither legally represented in court, nor permitted to consult a lawyer before their case was heard. Although some stated in court that they had pleaded guilty to the charges against them because they were tortured or intimidated, their allegations were not investigated. This is particularily serious because under Kenyan law appeals against conviction by defendants who have pleaded guilty are automatically rejected. In most cases defendants' guilty pleas or admissions were the only evidence against them. Further, the few lawyers prepared to take political cases have themselves suffered intimidation, and in one case, administrative detention under the Public Security Regulations.

The trials were public and held in the normal courts of first instance, the magistrates' courts, mainly in Nairobi before the Chief Magistrate, Mr H H Buch, the most senior trial magistrate. Most of the accused were charged with one or more of the following offences:

- "neglecting to report a felony" (Article 392 of the Penal Code), namely the existence of an anti-government organization publishing seditious publications: this is a misdemeanour, or minor offence, in the Penal Code, carrying a maximum sentence of two years' imprisonment - those convicted received prison sentences of between 15 and 18 months;

-"possession of a seditious publication" (Article 57 (2)), which carries a maximum sentence of seven years' imprisonment - those convicted were imprisoned for four or five years;

-"distribution of a seditious publication" (Article 57 (1)), which carries a maximum 10-year prison sentence - those convicted received five or six year prison sentences;

-"taking an unlawful oath" (Article 61), namely to join Mwakenya, which carries a maximum 10-year sentence - those convicted received four to six year prison sentences.

Four defendants were accused of communicating to a foreign power information prejudicial to the interests of Kenya, although Amnesty International has no precise details of the charges. Two defendants were charged with illegally possessing a weapon and three others were charged with sabotaging a railway line. No other defendants were charged with offences which specified the use or possible use or advocacy of violence.

All defendants pleaded guilty in court, except for three defendants

who initially pleaded not guilty and were then returned to custody: two
later changed their pleas and the third (who was charged in April 1987) was
still in custody at the time of writing. No defendant was permitted to
consult a lawyer before or during his trial. All were convicted and, with
three exceptions (where fines were imposed), were sentenced to prison
terms. Four and possibly more defendants appealed to the High Court against
their conviction or sentence but none of the appeals was successful. They
had a further right of appeal to the Court of Appeal but none of them is
known to have exercised this right.

Amnesty International does not have detailed information on all the
trials which have taken place. The organization's delegate observed two
trials (see Appendix I) but otherwise the only information has come from
reports in the Kenyan press (which are very brief and often lack basic
details of the precise charges), the official judgment record of the trial
or appeal and any details provided by observers who were present in court.
Full transcripts of trial proceedings are not kept in Kenya, the only
official record being the magistrate's short notes - which are only
available to lawyers for the purposes of making a judicial appeal.

Amnesty International has noted a pattern that has emerged in most, if
not all, of the trials, of which the following are the main elements:

-    prolonged periods of illegal, incommunicado and often unacknowledged
detention by the Special Branch during which prisoners alleged that they
were tortured or ill-treated;

-    the holding of trials unannounced in advance and outside normal court
schedules - consequently relatives or friends of the defendant were seldom
in court but police or Special Branch officers were normally present;

-    an extraordinary consistency of guilty pleas, alleged by some of those
convicted to have been made under duress;

-    the complete absence of lawyers at trials and denial of access to
lawyers during pre-trial detention;

-    the virtual absence of evidence against the defendants other than their
guilty pleas and admissions.

Virtually all the trials were judged by Chief Magistrate H H Buch,
with Assistant Deputy Public Prosecutor Bernard Chunga appearing for the
prosecution. As in all magistrate court trials, the magistrate sat alone
without jury or assessors.

The average length of each trial was about 30 minutes and the
proceedings followed the pattern of the two trials observed in December
1986 by Amnesty International's delegate (see Appendix I).

After the charges were read out the accused pleaded guilty. The
prosecution then read out a summary of the case and the defendant agreed
with this summary without, in most cases, questioning it. The defendant
then made a plea in mitigation - for example, explaining his family
situation, his regret and repentance, or mentioning a medical complaint -

after which the presiding magistrate delivered the verdict and sentence. The defendant was then given 14 days to appeal. At no point, to Amnesty International's knowledge, did the magistrate ask the defendant if he wanted legal representation and in no case did the magistrate comment on the obvious illegality of the defendant's having been detained well beyond the prescribed 24-hour time limit before being brought to court. After sentence the prisoner was transferred to an official prison where, for the first time since arrest, he was allowed to see his family and lawyer.

Joseph Kamonye Manje, a lecturer at the Kenya Science Teachers College in Nairobi, was one of the first people to be tried on charges of involvement with Mwakenya. He was arrested on 12 March 1986 at his home on the campus, brought to court on 2 April and charged with possession of a seditious publication. He was unrepresented and pleaded guilty. Assistant Deputy Public Prosecutor Bernard Chunga said that Joseph Kamonye Manje had admitted possession of "Mpatanishi No. 15", a Mwakenya publication, when his house was searched on 12 March. He told the court that the document had a seditious intent within the terms of Section 56 (1) (a), (b) and (c) of the Penal Code, namely "to overthrow by lawful means the Government of Kenya as by law established", "to excite the inhabitants of Kenya to attempt to procure the alteration otherwise than by unlawful means of any matter or thing in Kenya as by law established" and "to bring into hatred or contempt or to excite disaffection against the person of the President or the Government of Kenya as by law established".

The allegedly seditious document was produced in court but its contents were not disclosed. The prosecution went on to say that Joseph Kamonye Manje had admitted during the investigation that he and others not before the court had formed themselves into a group and had undertaken the printing and publication of the document. Joseph Kamonye Manje apparently admitted the prosecution summary of the case, which included no presentation of evidence or witnesses, but said no more apart from making a plea in mitigation expressing remorse and asking for leniency on the grounds of family responsibilities. He was convicted by Chief Magistrate Buch and sentenced to five years' imprisonment. He did not appeal.

Amnesty International is investigating allegations that Joseph Manje was tortured while held illegally and incommunicado for two weeks before his trial and that he may have pleaded guilty and made other admissions as a result of torture or duress.

Amnesty International has similar concerns about the trials of many others convicted subsequently, such as that of Oyangi Mbaja, manager of East African Spectre Ltd, a business owned by the former opposition leader Oginga Odinga. Oyangi Mbaja was arrested in Nairobi on 5 March 1986, held illegally and incommunicado for three weeks, then brought to trial to face the charge of "neglecting to report a felony". At his trial, where he was unrepresented, he pleaded guilty. The prosecuting counsel, Bernard Chunga, alleged that Oyangi Mbaja had met two men, Kariuki Gathitu and Geoffrey Maina, in Nairobi in July 1984 who had told him there was" a group of people that was not satisfied with the way the government was running". They were said to have showed him two of group's publications, which Oyangi Mbaja read and returned. The documents were alleged to be "Mpatanishi No.

Oyangi Mbaja
jailed for 30 months

Charles Kangara Njoroge
jailed for 15 months (see pp 12, 17)

15" and "Mwakenya". A copy of "Mpatanishi" was produced in court. Oyangi Mbaja denied having seen either document, saying that the document he had seen was another one (not produced in court), "Mpatanishi No. 12".

The case, however, continued with the prosecution stating that the document which Oyangi Mbaja had seen was seditious in that "it spelt out the group's intentions to bring into hatred or contempt or to incite disaffection against the Governmment of Kenya". Details about the document's contents were not disclosed. The prosecution also said that Oyangi Mbaja knew of the group's existence but had failed to report it to the authorities. Oyangi Mbaja made a plea in mitigation that he had refused to join or be a party to the group or its publications and that he was a life member of KANU, and "would not follow any group opposed to it". He made a plea for leniency on the grounds of family responsibilities. The magistrate convicted him and said Oyangi Mbaja was "sympathetic" to the group, even if he did not give it "total support". No evidence was apparently produced to support this. Oyangi Mbaja was sentenced to 30 months' imprisonment. It was mentioned at the trial that he had been imprisoned for sedition in 1971 and had served a seven year prison sentence. He did not appeal.

Julius Mwandawiro Mghanga, a former University of Nairobi student leader had been imprisoned for six months in 1985 for holding unlawful assemblies of students protesting against government actions against dissident students. He was arrested again on 1 April 1986 and held illegally and incommunicado until his trial on 29 April, at which he was not represented by a lawyer.

Julius Mwandawiro Mghanga, jailed for 5 years

Julius Mwandawiro Mghanga pleaded guilty to possession of a <u>Mwakenya</u> publication but in a mitigation plea said, "I have admitted the offence because of the intimidation and threats I received". Chief Magistrate Buch dismissed this statement as "an attempt by the former student leader to change his plea just before sentence was read out". He made no inquiry into the allegations of intimidation and sentenced to five years' imprisonment (<u>The Nation</u>, Nairobi, 30 April 1986).

At least four prisoners appealed to the High Court on the grounds that they had been wrongly convicted and/or given excessive sentences. Their convictions were all upheld, usually through a summary procedure, on the basis that the law does not allow an appeal against a guilty plea. Section 348 of the Criminal Procedure Code states: "No appeal shall be allowed in the case of any accused person who has pleaded guilty and has been convicted on such plea by a subordinate court, except as to the extent or legality of the sentence." None of the sentences was reduced on appeal.

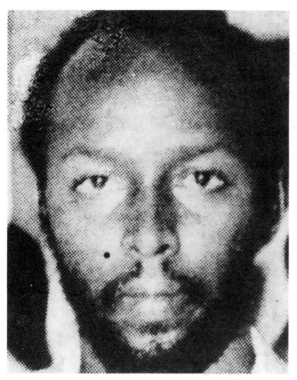 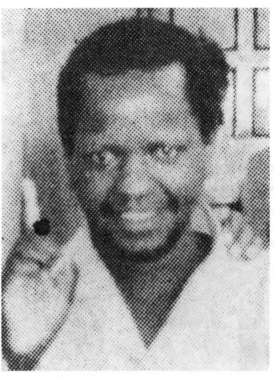

Wanderi Muthigani
jailed for 15 months

John Maina Kamangara, politician
jailed for 15 months

In one case, where Wanderi Muthigani, a former university student, alleged that he had pleaded guilty under duress, the judges, Mr Justice T Mbaluto and Mr Justice S E O Bosire, commented:

"The trial magistrate afforded the appellant the opportunity of being heard, first on plea to the charge, then in response to the facts which were outlined in support of the charge, and finally in mitigation of sentence . . . The appellant did not indicate to the trial court that he had either been tortured, intimidated or unduly influenced to admit the charge. The trial magistrate could not have guessed what was in the appellent's mind as to have refused to accept the guilty plea as not being genuine . . . It is only where exceptional circumstances are shown to have existed at the time of recording the pleas, which the court ought to have taken note of but did not do so, and which go to the root of the conviction, that an appellate court may vacate a conviction entered upon a guilty plea. We do not find any in the appellant's case. Accordingly we are satisfied that the appellant's plea of guilty was unequivocal."

The judges upheld the verdict and did not inquire into the torture allegations (High Court judgment, Muthigani vs. Republic, 8 November 1986).

A very important aspect of a fair trial is the right to consult and be represented by a lawyer. Article 14(3)(b) of the ICCPR, which the Government of Kenya ratified in 1972, provides that the accused in a criminal case shall have the right to "have adequate time and facilities for the preparation of his defence and to communicate with counsel of his choosing." Article 14(3)(d) states that the accused in a criminal case shall have the right to defend himself or herself "through legal assistance of his own choosing."

The right to defence counsel is enshrined in the constitution and laws of Kenya. According to Article 77(2) of the Constitution of Kenya, "every person who is charged with a criminal offence . . . (c) shall be given adequate time and facilities for the preparation of his defence; (d) shall be permitted to defend himself before the court in person or by a legal representative of his own choice. . . ." This right, however, was denied to the defendants in these trials.

Lawyers who had been consulted in the Mwakenya cases complained about the barriers which had been erected against their representation of people arrested on political charges. Some lawyers had been consulted by families of individuals who had "disappeared" after being arrested by the Special Branch. In addition to the difficulties of ascertaining a detainee's whereabouts or filing a habeas corpus application (see p9-10 above), lawyers had great difficulty in discovering when their client might be brought to court or were given misleading information.

When one lawyer learnt that his client had been brought to the Law Courts for an appearance that day he went to the Law Courts and told both Assistant Deputy Public Prosecutor Bernard Chunga and Chief Magistrate Buch's clerk that he was representing the accused. His client, in fact, was in a cell at the Law Courts, but the lawyer was not permitted to see him, and he was not presented in court that day. The lawyer's inquiries resulted in him being visited by a plainclothes police officer who warned him "not to take an interest in the case." His client was later brought to court two or three weeks after the arrest, when the lawyer was not present, pleaded guilty and was imprisoned. Convicted prisoners have also complained that when they asked to see a lawyer before their trial their requests were refused.

The most prominent lawyer in Kenya willing to represent political prisoners, Gibson Kamau Kuria, was himself arrested on 26 February 1987 at his law office in Nairobi. Despite appeals by the Law Society of Kenya to the authorities to explain the grounds for his arrest and clarify his whereabouts in custody, he "disappeared" after his arrest. A habeas corpus action was filed by his lawyer, Paul Muite, which resulted in the disclosure in court that he had been formally detained under Public Security Regulations under an order dated 6 March. The judge hearing the habeas corpus application appears to have not responded to his lawyer's complaint of unlawful detention prior to the issuance of the detention order. A further court judgement on 6 April stated merely that the detention was legal because an adminstrative detention order had been shown to the court.

Amnesty International believes that Gibson Kamau Kuria was arrested and detained solely on account of his professional legal activities on behalf of political prisoners. His case is similar to that of another lawyer, John Khaminwa, who, in 1982, was also one of the few lawyers who

*Gibson Kamau Kuria, lawyer and law lecturer
detained indefinitely without trial*

represented alleged government opponents or critics. John Khaminwa was detained without charge or trial after arguing in court that the government's use of detention without trial was unconstitutional. He was released in 1983.

Many lawyers informed Amnesty International's delegate during his visit to Nairobi in December 1986 that they were reluctant to take any political cases because they feared similiar reprisals. Gibson Kamau Kuria's subsequent arrest, "disappearance" and detention for an unspecified period without charge or trial would appear to confirm that such fears are justified. It also highlights the extent to which the authorities have sought to prevent Kenyans from exercising their legal rights. His detention has severely weakened the independence and effectivess of the legal profession in Kenya.

Amnesty International believes that this pattern of violation of legal rights provides sufficient evidence that these defendants did not receive fair trials in accordance with internationally recognized standards. The safeguards provided by the Constitution and laws of Kenya to prevent such violations of fundamental human rights appear to have been systematically undermined and rendered largely ineffective.

Amnesty International is also concerned that some of those convicted could be prisoners of conscience who were imprisoned because of their opinions, without having used or advocated violence (See Chapter 8).

7. DETENTION WITHOUT TRIAL

Since March 1986, 10 people have been detained for an indefinite period without charge or trial under Public Security (Detained and Restricted Persons) Regulations, 1978, made under the Preservation of Public Security Act. They were arrested on political grounds and are in most or all cases believed to have been accused of having links with Mwakenya. They were all held illegally, in excess of the 24-hour limit, before formal detention orders under Public Security Regulations were issued. There is no legal provision for holding suspects beyond 24 hours, without bringing them to court, other than under an administrative detention order under Public Security Regulations.

The abuse and ineffectiveness of the legal remedy for unlawful detention - habeas corpus - is illustrated by the case of Ngotho Kariuki, a former Dean of Commerce at the University of Nairobi. His detention was only acknowledged when a habeas corpus application by his family had been heard in court. In two other cases of unlawful detention, the detention orders against lawyers Mirugi Kariuki and Gibson Kamau Kuria were issued only after the court had ordered the police to produce the prisoners in court. The judges who heard these three cases did not comment on these extraordinary situations or on the fact that the prisoners were detained illegally before detention orders were issued. These cases suggest that administrative detention orders may have been imposed to punish their families for having sought their release.

Former prisoners have testified to being threatened by their interrogators with detention without trial as a worse punishment than a long prison sentence. It was said to be worse because it was indefinite and because of the harsh conditions under which administrative detainees are kept in Kenya. Prisoners alleged that they were told that detainees were denied medical treatment as a matter of official policy. While Amnesty International knows of no evidence that this is policy, it is the case that medical treatment for political detainees is often very poor and long delayed.

The imposition of detention orders must be announced in the official Kenya Gazette within two weeks. This procedure was apparently complied with in all cases. The standard notice of detention (see page 35) merely states that the detainee has been detained under Regulation 6 (1) of the Public Security (Detained and Restricted Persons) Regulations, 1978. No specific reason for the detention is publicly given. The act merely states that the Minister (that is, the Minister of State in the Office of the President who is responsible for internal security) may detain people on public security grounds. The detention notices were published under the name of the Permanent Secretary in the Office of the President.

The Constitution requires that detainees are given a written statement of the reasons for their detention within two weeks. It is not known if this is normally done, as no such statement has been published. However, The Standard newspaper in Nairobi appears to have had access to one such detention order or statement about the grounds of detention in the case of

Kariuki Gathitu, detained
indefinitely without trial

Katama Mkangi, detained
indefinitely without trial

the lawyer Gibson Kamau Kuria, when it reported that the official reasons
for his detention were his alleged involvement with Mwakenya and alleged
contacts with dissidents in exile. Anticipating that he was about to be
detained, Gibson Kamau Kuria had previously given a statement to a foreign
journalist denying any connection with Mwakenya or any subversive
organization. The accusation against him reported by The Standard did not
constitute a criminal charge nor does Gibson Kamau Kuria have any
opportunity to contest the allegations, which Amnesty International does
not find credible. Amnesty International believes that Gibson Kamau Kuria
was in fact detained because on several previous occasions and at the time
of his arrest he was acting on behalf of political prisoners. Most recently
- and this was probably the immediate cause of his arrest - he had begun
proceedings to sue the government on behalf of three political detainees
who were claiming that they had been detained unlawfully and tortured and
on behalf of the family of a fourth detainee who had died in custody.
Amnesty International believes that he was detained in order to stop these
legal actions. The organization has adopted him as a prisoner of conscience
imprisoned for his professional legal activities on behalf of political
prisoners.

In the other cases the authorities have given no reason for detaining
people under Public Security Regulations. However, in some later trials the
prosecution alleged that certain detainees held under Public Security
Regulations were also involved with Mwakenya. Amnesty International's
criticism of these trials (see Chapter 6) and the likelihood that many
defendants pleaded guilty and assented to the prosecution summary of the
facts of the case against them because of torture or duress makes it
doubtful whether any incriminating allegations made against other people

*Wanyiri Kihoro, lawyer
detained indefinitely without trial*

were true, especially when they concerned individuals who could not contest the allegations.

The Constitution requires that detainees or their lawyers must appear before a Detention Review Tribunal within one month of detention and thereafter at six monthly intervals. Detainees are granted access to their legal representative shortly before the review, but not usually on any other occasion.

The Detention Review Tribunal is headed by a High Court judge appointed, as are its other members, by the President. Detainees may make representations to the tribunal concerning their continuing detention and their conditions in detention (see Chapter 9). However, the tribunal's hearings are held in closed session and its reports are made confidentially to the Office of the President. Its findings are not binding on the Minister responsible for their detention or release. In the past, detainees' complaints about their treatment to the tribunal have rarely been attended to.

The 10 people detained under Public Security Regulations include the following five academics, all known for their critical views of the government:

Kariuki Gathitu, a lecturer in computer science;
Ngotho Kariuki , who had resigned from being Dean of Commerce at the University of Nairobi some years previously and worked as a tax consultant and lecturer in Tanzania, frequently visiting his family in Nairobi, where he had a publishing business;

Katama Mkangi, a lecturer in sociology;
Mukaru Ng'ang'a, a former lecturer in history who had not been re-employed by the university since his detention as a prisoner of conscience from 1982-84. He was arrested shortly before taking up a lecturership in Tanzania;
Gibson Kamau Kuria , a lecturer in law and also a practising lawyer (see above).

Two other lawyers have also been detained - Gibson Kamau Kuria had started legal proceedings against the government on their behalf shortly before he was detained, alleging that they had been unlawfully detained and tortured:

Mirugi Kariuki, a parliamentary candidate well known as a government critic, who has also represented political opponents of the government;
Wanyiri Kihoro, a former politician and known government critic who, earlier in 1986, had returned from the United Kingdom where he qualified in law and worked at the Africa Centre, an educational charity, in London;

The other three detainees are two former law students, previously identified as government critics, both of whom were detained for several months in 1982 - Gacheche wa Miano, and Patrick Ouma Onyango (a schoolteacher); and a manager of Oginga Odinga's business in Nairobi, East African Spectre Ltd, Israel Otieno Agina, who may have been detained because of his connection with the former Vice-President.

The authorities have had ample opportunity to bring these detainees to court if there is any evidence of their having committed a criminal offence. Amnesty International has received no response to its requests for information about the reasons for their detention and appeals for them to be charged with a recognizably criminal offence and given the benefit of fair trial in accordance with international standards or else released.

Amnesty International opposes the indefinite detention without trial of political prisoners. Furthermore, the information available to the organization about the reasons for the imprisonment of these 10 detainees and the failure of the authorities to charge them with any recognizable criminal offence involving the advocacy of violence has led it to conclude that they are prisoners of conscience detained on account of their non-violent opposition to the government.

8. PRISONERS OF CONSCIENCE

Amnesty International works for the immediate and unconditional release of prisoners of conscience. Prisoners of conscience are people who have been imprisoned because of their beliefs, colour, sex, ethnic origin, language or religion, who have not used or advocated violence.

It is Amnesty International's belief that some of the over 75 political prisoners who have been unfairly tried and convicted, as well as the 10 who are being detained indefinitely under Public Security Regulations, are prisoners of conscience.

The authorities have not stated the grounds on which they are holding the 10 detainees indefinitely without charge or trial under Public Security Regulations. They have not charged them with any recognizably criminal offence and clearly do not intend to do so. They have given them no opportunity to challenge any accusations that may have been made against them - for example, that they are linked to Mwakenya. Amnesty International has received no response to its inquiries into the precise reasons for their detention or to its call for them to be released if they are not to be charged with a recognizably criminal offence and given a fair trial in accordance with international standards. As explained in the previous chapter, Amnesty International believes they have been imprisoned for their non-violent opinions and has adopted them as prisoners of conscience.

Amnesty International has been investigating whether some of those imprisoned after trial and conviction on political charges are prisoners of conscience. The organization is also concerned that they did not receive fair trials and that their guilty pleas and acceptance of the prosecution's summary of the case against them may have been extracted through torture or other duress. In no case did the prosecution produce witnesses or other independent evidence against the accused or introduce written statements from the accused as evidence. In most cases Amnesty International believes that the prosecution case against most of them was not proved beyond any reasonable doubt and did not overcome the presumption of their innocence.

Many of those brought to court were charged with sedition-related offences. Amnesty International is concerned that the law against sedition in Kenya (Articles 56 and 57 of the Penal Code) does not clearly distinguish between violent and non-violent criticism of or opposition to the government and thus does not adequately protect the right to hold, express and disseminate non-violent opinions. The law has been used in the past to imprison prisoners of conscience. Maina wa Kinyatti, a history lecturer adopted by Amnesty International as a prisoner of conscience, is currently serving a six-year sentence imposed in 1982 for allegedly possessing a leaflet which criticized the government but did not advocate violence against it.

In the case of those convicted of sedition during the past year, the nature of the alleged sedition was not made clear in court. Reference was simply made to the law, and principally to the law's definition of a "seditious intention" (see page 27). They were charged with offences such as failing to report having seen a seditious organization's publication, possessing or distributing such a document, or taking an oath to join such an organization - offences removed by varying degrees from the commission of any seditious act or any act involving the use or advocacy of politically-motivated violence. Whether or not the organization alleged to have published such leaflets had advocated or used violence against the government was not specified in court.

In the trials of over 20 defendants charged with "neglecting to report a felony" (Article 392), the prosecution apparently intended to penalise the defendant's alleged contact with the publications or members of a seditious organization (Mwakenya). However, on the basis of the charge alone such contact cannot be deemed sufficient evidence of their involvement with the organization. The mere failure to report to the authorities the existence of the organization's publications (particularly since the authorities obviously knew about it, certainly from the time of the first arrests and trials in March 1986 and probably even before that) cannot on its own be regarded in any way as evidence of advocacy of the organization's objectives. Those convicted solely on this charge are therefore regarded by Amnesty International as prisoners of conscience.

Amnesty International also believes that the over 20 defendants convicted of "possession of a seditious publication" (Article 56) are prisoners of conscience. The mere possession of a publication is not evidence of advocacy of the views contained in it, unless the circumstances of possession were proved in a fair trial to demonstrate the defendant's advocacy of the views expressed in the publication.

The charge against more than 10 defendants, of "distribution of a seditious publication" (Article 56), indicates a closer connection between the defendants and the publication they were said to be distributing. Amnesty International is investigating the cases of those convicted of this offence in order to determine whether they received fair trials as well as whether or not they personally advocated violence or whether the publication they were alleged to have distributed advocated violence.

The contents of the allegedly seditious publications were not disclosed in court in any of these trials. Although the documents were given to the presiding magistrates the latter refused to allow disclosure of their contents on the grounds that they were patently seditious and prejudicial to national security. Neither the prosecution nor the magistrate mentioned whether or not the publication advocated violence. The publications concerned were "Mpatanishi", "Pambana", "Mzalendo ", "Minutes of the First Mwakenya Congress", "Draft Mwakenya Program", and other publications of Mwakenya or a previously formed opposition organization, the "December Twelfth Movement". No evidence was presented to prove that the documents had any "seditious intention". The authorities have not replied to Amnesty International's requests for clarification of whether or not any of the documents advocated violence. On the basis of an examination of one of the documents, "Mzalendo", it appears that the advocacy of violence was added to Mwakenya's objectives in early 1986, whereas its objectives may have been previously non-violent. Amnesty International is not, however, able currently to verify whether or not the other publications cited in the trials advocated violence or not.

Over 20 defendants were charged with "taking an unlawful oath" (Article 61). This charge implied that they were members of a seditious organization (Mwakenya). (No defendant has been charged with "membership of an illegal organization" and, indeed, neither Mwakenya nor any other clandestine opposition organization with the same or similar views has been officially proscribed or banned). A person taking such an oath of allegiance, in whatever cultural manner it was taken, could be regarded as sharing the principal stated objectives of the organization, although not necessarily approving of all its objectives or actions. Defendants convicted of this charge in a fair trial when there was no clear evidence of their disavowal of violence, would not be eligible for adoption by Amnesty International as prisoners of conscience if the organization to which they were accused of belonging clearly used or advocated violence.

In April 1987 four former University of Nairobi students were brought to court and accused of giving information to a foreign power, the Libyan embassy in Nairobi, which was prejudicial to the interests of Kenya. They were sentenced to prison terms ranging from 15 months to 10 years. They were alleged to have provided information about political opposition to the Kenyan government, apparently in exchange for obtaining scholarships to study in Libya. The Kenyan Government also made public allegations that Kenyan dissidents were receiving military training in Libya and expelled five Libyan diplomatic representatives from the country on the grounds that they had been in contact with the accused in these trials. Precise details of the charges against the four former students are not known to Amnesty International, which is investigating whether they may have been imprisoned for their political opinions.

In conclusion, Amnesty International believes that the prosecution did not adequately establish in the majority of cases that those convicted of political offences had advocated violence. Amnesty International is continuing to investigate their cases and considers that many among them are or may be prisoners of conscience, imprisoned solely for their non-violent political opinions or activities.

9. PRISON CONDITIONS

Political prisoners are held in harsh conditions, both while in Special Branch custody after their arrest, and in official prisons after their convictions or detentions under Public Security Regulations.

Special Branch Custody

After arrest people suspected of supporting Mwakenya have usually been held for a few hours in a police station before being transferred to Special Branch custody for interrogation. The treatment of prisoners held by the Special Branch for investigation and their conditions of imprisonment in Nyayo House have already been described (Chapter 4). Prisoners' testimonies indicate a systematic pattern of torture and intimidation and harsh conditions of detention. Prisoners are held incommunicado, without official acknowledgement, and are denied medical treatment. The death of Peter Njenga Karanja in Special Branch custody on 26 February 1987 apparently as a result of torture and denial of medical treatment is a case in point.

Convicted Prisoners

Those prisoners subsequently taken to court and convicted of a political offence are then transferred to an official prison to serve their sentences, alongside other convicted prisoners. They have no special status as "political prisoners". Amnesty International has learnt that some political prisoners were informed early in their prison term that they would not be granted the one-third remission of sentence for good behaviour to which Section 46 of the Prisons Act entitles all prisoners. No explanation was given.

Political prisoners suffer harsh conditions. They sleep on the cold cement floor of their cells, without a bed, and with only sleeping mats and blankets. They wear the prison uniform of shorts, short-sleeved shirt and rubber sandals. A sweater is not always allowed, although the climate can be extremely cold in some prisons. In other prisons, it is sometimes extremely hot. Prisoners are allowed monthly family visits and access to lawyers on request, and can write a certain number of letters to relatives each month. These provisions are, however, not always adhered to. Prisoners are permitted medical treatment through the Prison Medical Service, with hospital admission in serious cases, but many prisoners are said to have had difficulty in obtaining satisfactory qualified medical treatment. Prisoners do prison work, which may involve prison cleaning, tailoring, or, if transferred to a rural prison, agricultural labour. The latter can be particularly arduous. Amnesty International has received reports of extremely harsh conditions suffered by university students held in various prisons after being convicted of political offences in 1985. They said they were held in extremely insanitary conditions, and suffered considerable brutality from prison officials.

Public Security Detainees

Those detained under Public Security Regulations are treated differently to convicted political prisoners. They are held under different prison rules, do no work, and are not granted the same rights as other prisoners. The prison where they are held is not disclosed. They are often held in permanent solitary confinement.They are allowed family visits very rarely, sometimes only once a year and usually not in the prison where they are held. They are only given access to lawyers before their six-monthly appearances before the Detention Review Tribunal. Their letters are delayed for two or three months, which deprives their families of knowledge of their condition or health. Families often attempt to send books, clothing, medicines or other items to the detainees but on past evidence these are either not delivered by the authorities or are held for some months before they are given to the prisoner. Some detainees have not been allowed to have any books at all during years of detention, and in some cases have not even been allowed to read the Bible or Quran.

Detainees receive worse medical treatment than convicted prisoners. They are often denied medical treatment until their condition is extremely serious. Several detainees are suspicious of the medical treatment given. No information on their health is usually given to their families. Their diet is poor and they are allowed very little exercise or fresh air. Medical recommendations for their diet are often ignored. Like convicted political prisoners, they wear prison uniform and have no bed or mattress to sleep on.

Public Security detainees are usually held in maximum security prisons, such as Kamiti prison in Nairobi, Shimo-la-Tewa prison in Mombasa, Hola prison in northeastern Kenya, Manyani prison near Voi, or Naivasha prison (see map). The Mombasa prison is notorious for its heat, humidity and malarial mosquitoes; the Hola prison for heat. Detainees are usually transferred to Shimo-la-Tewa prison in Mombasa for Detention Review Tribunal hearings.

Amnesty International has not received reports of detainees having been tortured after they have been served with detention orders and transferred to official prisons, although conditions there are very harsh. Some prisoners are reported to have suffered nervous breakdowns as a result. On several occasions in the past and at least twice during 1987, detainees are reported to have undertaken hunger strikes in protest against their conditions or their transfer to a particular prison, or against their being held indefinitely without charge or trial.

10. AMNESTY INTERNATIONAL'S RECOMMENDATIONS TO THE GOVERNMENT OF KENYA

In January 1987 Amnesty International made a number of recommendations to
President Daniel arap Moi concerning prisoners of conscience, torture, the
"disappearance" and unlawful detention of political prisoners,
administrative detention without trial, and prison conditions of political
prisoners. No response was received and the recommended measures have not
been implemented. The following is a more detailed, public presentation of
the measures which Amnesty International believes to be essential to
protect fundamental human rights in Kenya.

10.1 Prisoners of Conscience

Amnesty International has appealed for the immediate and unconditional
release of all prisoners of conscience imprisoned solely for their non-
violent opinions. In particular, Amnesty International has called for the
immediate and unconditional release of Gibson Kamau Kuria, a lawyer
imprisoned for his professional legal activities on behalf of political
prisoners.

Other prisoners of conscience for whose release Amnesty International
is working include people detained for an indefinite period without trial
under Public Security Regulations, as well as certain prisoners convicted
of political offences where there is no evidence that they had used or
advocated violence. Amnesty International is investigating many other cases
of convicted political prisoners in order to determine whether they could
be prisoners of conscience. It has asked the authorities to review the
cases of all people imprisoned after being convicted of political offences
in order to ensure that no-one is imprisoned for his or her non-violent
opinions.

10.2 Unlawful Custody and "Disappearances"

Amnesty International has urged that all persons arrested on political
grounds should be brought to court within the 24 hour period stipulated by
law or otherwise released unconditionally. The government should ensure
that all prisoners are allowed prompt access to their relatives and legal
representative and that the whereabouts of all those arrested are made
known to their families, legal representative or members of the public. An
accurate and up-to-date central register should be kept of all people
arrested, as well as registers at particular places of custody, such as
police stations, and these registers should be open to public inspection.
Secret detention outside the framework of the law by the Special Branch or
any other security agency should be strictly forbidden.

All prisoners and their families should be given adequate opportunity
to challenge before a court the legality of and reasons for detention, if
the prisoner is held beyond the prescribed 24 hour period without being
brought to court. Judges should assert their responsibility to ensure that
the remedy of habeas corpus for unlawful or abusive detention is effective.

Whenever prisoners are charged with political offences, the magistrate should specifically inquire into the legality of the prisoner's detention prior to trial, in order to investigate whether this met with the requirements of the law. When not satisfied that the legal requirements were observed, the magistrate should order an investigation with a view to establishing if the detention was unlawful and the detaining authorities had therefore committed a criminal offence. Magistrates and judges must demonstrate their determination to uphold the law in this particular respect.

When a prisoner is reported to have "disappeared" after being arrested in circumstances which indicate that the arrest was politically motivated, the authorities should immediately investigate what has happened to the prisoner, which agency was responsible for the arrest, which agency is holding him or her, where, under what conditions and for what reasons. Immediate and urgent steps should be taken to have the prisoner produced before a court to make sure that he or she has not been ill-treated so that the court can obtain an explanation for his/her detention and legal status. The government must publicly declare its determination to ensure that "disappearances" do not take place.

10.3 Safeguards against Torture

By acceding to the International Covenant on Civil and Political Rights in 1972 the Government of Kenya has pledged its support for Article 7 which states: "No one shall be subjected to torture or to cruel, inhuman or degrading treatment or punishment."

In its Declaration on the Protection of all Persons from Torture and other Cruel, Inhuman or Degrading Treatment or Punishment, adopted on 9 December 1975, the United Nations' General Assembly condemned torture as an offence to human dignity and said that no state may permit or tolerate it. The General Assembly called on every state to take effective measures "to prevent torture and other cruel, inhuman or degrading treatment or punishment from being practised within its jurisdiction."

Torture is more likely to occur when prisoners are held incommunicado or in secret, without access to relatives, lawyers or doctors, often without charge and without being brought before a judicial authority such as a magistrate or judge. All these conditions prevail in Kenya as far as people in the custody of the Special Branch are concerned. Numerous allegations of torture have been made by people who were later freed without charge, people who were later detained indefinitely without trial, and people who were later taken to court and charged.

Amnesty International's appeal to the Government of Kenya to stop torture and protect prisoners in the future from being tortured include the following recommendations:

1. Official Condemnation of Torture

The head of state and senior members of the government and the security forces should demonstrate publicly their total opposition to torture and should instruct all officers responsible for holding or interrogating prisoners, including Special Branch personnel and the various branches of the police and the armed forces, that torture is unlawful and will not be tolerated under any circumstances.

2. Limits on Incommunicado Custody

The government should adopt safeguards to ensure that incommunicado custody is not an opportunity for torture. All those arrested should be promptly brought before a magistrate or other judicial authority, and relatives, legal counsel and medical personnel should have immediate and regular access to them.

3. No Secret or Illegal Custody or "Disappearances" of Prisoners

Relatives and legal counsel should be informed promptly of the whereabouts of people who have been arrested; no-one should be held in secret or unacknowledged custody. Those responsible for administering the law should assert their authority to ensure that the maximum period of custody without charge allowed by law (24 hours) is not exceeded. All prisoners should be given adequate opportunity to challenge both the legality of and the reasons for their custody before a court and should be released immediately if their custody is not lawful. The remedy of habeas corpus for unlawful custody should be made effective.

4. Safeguards during Interrogation and Custody

All prisoners should be informed of their right to lodge complaints with the courts about torture or ill-treatment. Those concerned with the administration of law and justice should assert their special responsiblities for assuring the well-being of detainees. People arrested should not be held in the custody of the same branch of the police as the one which is responsible for their interrogation. There should be regular inspections of places of custody and interrogation, particularly those places where torture has been frequently reported, to ensure that torture does not take place and that prisoners are not subjected to torture or other cruel, inhuman or degrading treatment. Such inspections should include visits by government and judicial officials, national bodies and relevant international humanitarian organizations such as the International Committee of the Red Cross.

5. Independent Investigations of Reports of Torture

The Government should ensure that an impartial body investigates all complaints and reports of torture. Its findings and methods of investigation should be made public.

6. No Admissibility in Court of Guilty Pleas or Statements extracted under Torture

Steps should be taken to ensure that confessions, statements or pleas of guilty which were obtained through torture or threats of torture may never be invoked in legal proceedings or used to justify the imprisonment of detainees. Both subordinate and appellate courts should be particularly careful in examining pleas of guilty made by defendants while in custody - particularly if they had been held illegally and without access to defence counsel, in order to verify that they were not made under torture. If allegations of torture are made in court the judge must order that the allegations are impartially investigated. Whenever there is reason to suspect that defendants were coerced into making guilty pleas, they should be retried.

7. Prosecution of Alleged Torturers

When there is evidence that an act of torture had been committed by or at the instigation of a public official, criminal proceedings for torture should be instituted against the alleged offender.

8. Training Procedures

It should be made clear during the training of all officials involved in the custody, interrogation or treatment of prisoners that torture is a crime. They should be instructed that they are obliged to refuse to obey any order to torture.

9. Compensation and Rehabilitation

Victims of torture and their dependents should be entitled to obtain financial compensation. Victims should also be provided with appropriate medical care or rehabilitation.

10.4 Indefinite Administrative Detention without Trial

Amnesty International has appealed for all those arrested on political grounds for reasons other than their non-violent opinions to be either formally charged with a recognizably criminal offence and tried in accordance with international standards of fair trial, or else released. The organization opposes the indefinite detention of political prisoners without charge or trial and calls for a review of the Preservation of Public Security Act, and the repeal of its provisions for detention without trial.

10.5 Fair Trial

Amnesty International has appealed to the government to ensure that all those tried for political offences are given fair trials in accordance with recognized international standards of fair trial. The following points have been stressed:

1. The Right to Legal Counsel

Those arrested should be given the opportunity to consult with a lawyer of their choice as soon as possible after arrest. Lawyers should be permitted immediate access to their clients after arrest in order to prepare for proceedings. The authorities should not threaten people under arrest or their families with any sanction as a result of their wish to consult a lawyer. Nor should any lawyer be threatened with reprisals or suffer any persecution on account of being prepared to represent a client arrested on political grounds.

When people brought to court on political charges are not legally represented Amnesty International recommends that magistrates specifically inquire into whether they wish to be legally represented and that they ensure that defendants are provided with the assistance of a legal representative of their choice whenever there is any indication that they so desire.

2. Pleas

When defendants in political cases plead guilty, Amnesty International recommends that magistrates examine whether the plea was made voluntarily. If, at any stage of the trial proceedings, it is alleged that the defendant suffered duress, ill-treatment or torture, Amnesty International recommends that the magistrate opens a formal investigation into the allegation and takes whatever steps might be appropriate to protect the complainant from any reprisal by the detaining authority against whom the complaint was made. Amnesty International further recommends such investigation even at the stage of appeal to a higher court, even if the defendant has pleaded guilty.

Where a guilty plea or admission of the case presented by the prosecution is shown to have been made as a result of duress, such pleas or admissions should be ruled inadmissible.

3. Retrial

Amnesty International recommends a detailed review by an impartial judicial body of all the above-mentioned trials of people convicted of political offences since March 1986. In view of the serious breaches of internationally recognized standards of fair trial in virtually all the trials, to the extent that the accused could not reasonably be said to have received a fair trial or to have been fairly convicted; Amnesty International recommends that all the convicted prisoners should be retried in accordance with international standards of fair trial.

10.6 Treatment of Prisoners

Amnesty International recommends that the Government of Kenya take steps to ensure that the UN Standard Minimum Rules for the Treatment of Prisoners are respected. In particular, Amnesty International urges that all political prisoners are allowed the following basic rights:

- immediate access to legal representatives and further access whenever required for their legal representation or other legal business;

- immediate and regular visits from their families and regular correspondence wiith them;
- ready access to professional medical attention, with hospital admission when required, and the provision of medically prescribed diets;
- regular access to spiritual representatives, religious reading material and worship;
- provision of nutritionally adequate diet and acceptable standards of hygiene;
- provision of books and other reading and writing materials and access to newspapers and news broadcasts, or permission to receive these from families and permission to study or follow study courses and take examinations;
- regular provision of information from the authorities to their families on their whereabouts, conditions and treatment, particularly their health and medical treatment;
- the opportunity for regular exercise and recreation.

10.7 Ratification of International Human Rights Instruments

In addition to the International Covenants on Civil and Political Rights and on Economic, Social and Cultural Rights, to which Kenya acceded in 1972, Amnesty International recommends that the Government of Kenya also accede to the following international and regional human rights instruments, as a demonstration of commitment to the protection of human rights in the country and of its desire to ensure respect for recognized international human rights standards:

- the African Charter on Human and Peoples' Rights;
- the Optional Protocol to the International Covenant on Civil and Political Rights;
- the Convention against Torture and Other Cruel, Inhuman or Degrading Treatment or Punishment.

48

APPENDIX I
TWO TRIAL OBSERVATIONS BY AN AMNESTY INTERNATIONAL DELEGATE, PROFESSOR
DAVID WEISSBRODT, PROFESSOR OF LAW, UNIVERSITY OF MINNESOTA, USA

1. The Trial of Vitalis Owinyo Agutu

On 17 December 1986 at 2:45 pm the normal business of Chief Magistrate Mr H. H. Buch, had been completed. In Courtroom No. 5 of the Law Courts, where the Chief Magistrate ordinarily presides, there were three uniformed guards, two plainclothes officers from the Criminal Investigation Department (CID), four plainclothes Special Branch officers, one member of the public, the Chief Magistrate's clerk at his desk just under the Chief Magistrate's high desk, four newspaper reporters, the Assistant Deputy Public Prosecutor, Bernard Chunga, the Amnesty International observer, and the accused handcuffed in the dock flanked by two uniformed police officers.

The Chief Magistrate entered the room and everyone rose. The clerk called out the name of the first accused, Vitalis Owinyo Agutu, and he rose. The clerk asked whether the accused wanted to proceed in English or Swahili. The accused said, "Swahili". Translation into English or Swahili was made throughout the trial.

Clerk: "Count one of the accusation is that the accused is charged with having taken an oath in September 1985 to join a seditious organization (contrary to Section 61 of the Penal Code). The second count is that the accused was aware of the commission of a felony, which was the distribution of a seditious publication in violation of Article 57(1)(c) of the Penal Code, and failed to report that felony to the authorities or to otherwise prevent the commission of the felony, which constitutes a violation of Article 392 of the Penal Code. Are these charges true or not true?"

Accused: "True."

The prosecuting counsel, Mr Bernard Chunga, who is the Assistant Deputy Public Prosecutor, then rose from his seat in the front row before the Chief Magistrate. He began speaking at 2:46 pm with translation in Swahili by the clerk:

"The basic facts are those which relate to the charges which have just been read. I wish to add only the following facts. The accused was born in 1948. He attended primary education for two to three years. Then he dropped out. He went to Mombasa to find work and worked for a shop. He found a job with the East African Railways and Harbours. He worked as a labourer for the railways in Mombasa, Nakuru and Gilgil. He continued working for the railways up to the time of his arrest on 4 December 1986. While at the Mombasa Railway Station in March 1981, Agutu was approached by another employee of the railway. The other employee was working as the assistant station master at Nakuru Station. The employee informed the accused that there was a secret party or organization called "the December 12th Movement" formed to fight and overthrow the Government of Kenya. The employee informed the accused that the secret organization had printed or published some leaflets called Pambana which were to be distributed as a method of educating the masses about the object of the secret organization. The employee asked the accused to assist in the distribution of the pamphlets. In April 1981 and July 1981 the accused, along with others, distributed pamphlets in four different parts of the Nakuru area. The accused also participated in the production of seditious publications of the secret organization for propagating the organization's objectives and ideas.

"In 1983 the same employee of the railway, who had earlier informed the accused about the secret organization, told the accused that the December 12th Movement had changed its name to 'Mwakenya'. The objectives of the secret organization remained the same, namely, to fight and overthrow the government. Subsequently, the accused continued his briefings with the employee and in September 1985 the employee called upon the accused at the accused's home at 8:00 pm in the evening. The employee drove the accused to a place in Nakuru district. The employee led the accused to a certain house where the accused, without being compelled, took an oath to compound or cement his membership and to bind himself to the secret organization, which was originally the December 12th Movement and which was then the Mwakenya organization. Apart from the accused, there were five or six others who took the oath on that occasion. The oath was done secretly at night. When his time came, the accused entered the home and was asked to take a chair. He was given a horn with a liquid in it. He was asked to and did sip the liquid in the horn. There was someone administering the oath in the house who pierced the accused's body on the neck. As the blood came out, the accused was asked to repeat certain words to the effect that the accused was strong for Mwakenya.

"The above facts are the prosecution case constituting the first count of the charges against the accused. The accused was not compelled to take the oath. The accused was binding himself to the Mwakenya movement, whose objectives the accused knew at the time to be seditious. The accused's oath was to bind him to a seditious organization. Those facts constitute the first count.

"Count 2 is founded upon the same facts as Count 1. The accused was made aware as from March or May 1981 of the existence of a secret organization, of the seditious purposes of the organization, and of the purposes of the organization to distribute seditious pamphlets. The accused did help with the distribution of the pamphlets. The accused never reported these matters to the police or to any government institution for the purpose of preventing the crime. It is a felony under Section 57(1)(c) of the Penal Code to distribute a seditious publication. The accused was aware of the desire to commit this felony and therefore committed the offence of failing to prevent this felony, which is the charge against him. These are the basic facts against the accused and these facts prove the charge."

Mag: "Does he admit?"

Accused: "Yes."

Clerk: "Yes, he admits."

Pros: "The accused is a first offender."

[At this point three members of the public began to enter the court-room. The Chief Magistrate was annoyed at this interruption and ordered that the three individuals be removed from the courtroom. The closest uniformed guard stopped the three individuals from entering more than three metres into the courtroom. The guard removed the individuals from the room.]

Pros: "Except for his arrest on 4 December, the accused has not previously been arrested. The prosecution asks the court to take into account the facts as they appear on the record. The facts are that he was aware of a felony and he did not take any action to prevent the felony."

Clerk: "Do you have anything to say?"

Accused: "I ask the court to excuse me under God. Let me see my family. I am married: I have two wives and 10 children. One of my children is ill. I was born in an agricultural area. The kids are depending on me. My mother and father are still alive; they are old. My mother broke a hip bone and she can do nothing, according to the instructions of her doctor. I also have four brothers who depend on me. So I ask the court to forgive me. My whole family depends on me. I would like to tell the court that I am handicapped; my hand was broken in an accident [prior to his arrest]. Since I was arrested on December 4th, my family does not know where I am. If I do get sentenced to prison, please sentence me to a prison in my area. I don't want to be in a prison far from home."

Mag: (after three minutes' silence, taking notes in the file) "You are sentenced to four years on the first count and 18 months on the second count. The two sentences will run concurrently. You have 14 days in which to use your right to appeal."

One of the uniformed guards removed the accused from the dock and the accused was taken out of the front door of the courtroom [3.15 pm].

2. The Trial of Bernard Wachira Waheire

Just after the first prisoner had left the courtroom, another accused was brought up the steps behind the dock, Bernard Wachira Waheire.

Clerk: [at 3:16 pm] "Bernard Wachira Waheire, do you want to use English or Swahili?"

Accused: "English."

Clerk: "Count one of the accusation is that the accused is charged with having taken an oath in 1985 to a seditious organization, which constitutes a violation of Article 61 of the Penal Code. Is that true or not true?"

Accused: "It is true."

Clerk: "The second count is that the accused was aware of the commission of a felony, which was the distribution of a seditious publication in violation of Article 57(1)(c) of the Penal Code and failed to report that felony to the authorities or to otherwise prevent the commission of the felony, which constitutes a violation of Article 392 of the Penal Code. Is this true or not true?"

Accused: "True."

Pros: (Mr Bernard Chunga, Assistant Deputy Public Prosecutor) [at 3.17 pm]: "The basic facts are as read out in the charges. The accused was born in 1959. In 1979 he went to the University of Nairobi. He graduated in 1984. Prior to graduation, he had been shown, had read, and understood a Pambana publication. That was in 1982, shortly before the coup of 1 August 1982. Having completed university, the accused became a commercial assistant in a commercial firm, where he was working up to December 2, 1986, the day of arrest. While working with the private firm, the accused in February 1985 was approached by an old university colleague. That university colleague informed the accused there was an organization which had been secretly formed to fight and overthrow the Government of Kenya. The old colleague said the organization was named 'Mwakenya'. The old colleague asked the accused to join it. The accused asked for time. Around August 1985 the same old colleague of the university invited the accused for an evening drink in a bar in Nairobi. The accused went to the bar and found the colleague and two others. The conversation was about the secret organization; the accused was informed that the organization had backing abroad. The accused was asked to join the organization. He was asked whether he had seen the tract, Mpatanishi. He said that he had not seen it. He was told that he would not be permitted to read the document unless he became a member, that is, unless he was 'oathed' as a member. He should give a financial contribution to the organization. The accused agreed and gave 40 shillings as a first contribution.

"Subsequent to this meeting, the accused had another occasion to meet the old university colleague. The accused was taken to a home in the Umoja Estate [in Nairobi]. Without being compelled, the accused took an oath purporting to bind the accused to the secret organization Mwakenya. He was given a liquid substance which he drank and he took an oath that he would remain loyal to the secret organization. He bound himself to the organization's objectives. The oath was unlawful and was secretly taken in the night. After the ceremony, the accused was taken back to his house and promised a copy of the Mpatanishi document to make himself familiar with the organization's purposes. In September 1985 the accused went on a course sponsored by his employer. At the course he met another old university colleague who gave him a copy of the document Mpatanishi no. 14. The accused read the document and understood the organization's purposes. Hence, the accused took an unlawful oath binding the accused to a secret organization, Mwakenya, which is the prosecution case. The unlawful oath was not compelled. The purpose of the oath was to engage the accused in a seditious enterprise, that is, to overthrow the government. That is the subject of the first count.

"The second count is based upon the same facts. The accused was made aware of the distribution of the Pambana pamphlet as far back as May 1982, which he was shown and a copy of which he read. After graduating, he met an old colleague who informed him of the organization's existence and of its seditious purposes. Finally, the accused became aware of the publication and distribution of Mwakenya publications. The accused did not report these activities to the police or to any lawful authority or institution. The accused did not use any means to prevent the publication of these seditious documents, which constitute a felony under Article 57(1)(c) of the Penal Code. These facts are the subject of the second count." [3:31 pm]

Mag: (after writing notes in the file, at 3.31 pm): "Does the accused understand and agree?"

Clerk: "Do you understand and agree?"

Accused:"Yes, your honour."

Pros: "The accused is a first offender. His first arrest occurred on December 2nd. The court should take into account the length of time which the accused was possessed of knowledge of seditious documents without reporting it. Also, the accused took an oath with seditious purposes."

Clerk: "Do you want to say something?"

Accused:"I am the last boy of my mother, who is old. I was misled into these activities. I was interested in getting married. I have a small daughter. I have loan obligations, which no one will be able

to handle if I am sentenced. My family will suffer if I am put in
jail.   Also,   I am sorry for having taken part. That's all, your
honour." [3:35 pm]

(Silence; the Chief Magistrate writes in the file.)

Mag: "On count one the accused is sentenced to four years. On count two
the sentence is 18 months. The sentences will run concurrently.
The accused has a right of appeal within 14 days against the
sentence."

The Chief Magistrate left the courtroom at 3:38 pm.

3.   Notes

1.   The delegate also observed several hours of court proceedings that
day involving criminal and not political cases, both before and
after the proceedings described above. He sat in the public area
of the courtroom and the proceedings were at least formally open to
the public, even if they occurred at an unusual hour. After the
two trials above, he introduced himself to the Chief Magistrate and
to the prosecuting counsel.

The two trials described above differed from other trials observed
that day in several respects. The trials were held at an unusual
time   of   the courtroom schedule and apparently without the
defendants' families being informed. The first defendant stated
that his family had no knowledge of what had happened to him since
his arrest. If there was any public announcement of the trials, it
was minimal.   The defendants' families were absent, neither
defendant had a legal representative, and hardly any members of the
public were present.

2.   The Nation newspaper report of the trials is appended below. As in
most reports of political trials in 1986-87, the reports are brief
and omit several significant details. They are, however, in most
cases the only information publicly available on the trial, due to
the absence of legal representatives, families or friends of the
defendant. As with most, if not all the trials, there were no
foreign correspondents present.

3.   Press report of the trials - "Two get 4 years for sedition" (The
Nation, 18 December 1986)

Two men were jailed for four years each yesterday for taking
unlawful oaths to join a clandestine movement in Kenya and for
failing to report the existence of the movement. Vitalis Owinyo
Agutu of Kenya Railways admitted he took the oath at Ngachura in
Nakuru while Bernard Wachira Waheire,a commercial assistant with a
private Nairobi firm, took the oath at Umoja Estate, Nairobi. The
two pleaded with the Chief Magistrate, Mr. H.H. Buch,for leniency
and said they were remorseful. They said they were misled into
joining the movement. The Assistant Deputy Public Prosecutor, Mr.
Bernard Chunga, told the court that Agutu went to school for three

years and then joined the then East African Railways and Harbours. He worked in Mombasa, Nakuru and Gilgil. When he was arrested, Agutu (38), was working as a labourer at the Nakuru station. The court heard that in 1981 the station's assistant master had approached Agutu and told him of a secret organisation called December Twelve Movement which had been formed to overthrow the Government. He also learnt that the movement was printing and distributing a seditious publication called "Pambana". In August last year, Waheire was approached by a friend who informed him that the clandestine movement had support from Kenyans abroad. Waheire agreed to join them. He was taken to a house at Umoja Estate where he took the oath. Like Agutu, he did not report the matter to the authorities, the court heard. Agutu and Waheire were jailed for four years each for taking the unlawful oath and 18 months for failing to report the felony. The sentences are to run concurrently.

They were given 14 days to appeal.

APPENDIX II
PEOPLE DETAINED UNDER PUBLIC SECURITY REGULATIONS FROM 1986 TO JUNE 1987

Name	Arrest Date (Y/M/D)	Detention Date (Y/M/D)	Personal Details
AGINA Israel Otieno	86/08/29	86/12/09	Businessman, manager of East African Spectre Ltd
GATHITU Kariuki	86/03/05	86/03/26	Lecturer, Institute of Computer Science, University of Nairobi; M.Sc, University of Dundee, Scotland, 1985
KARIUKI Mirugi	86/12/09	86/12/22	Lawyer and politician
KARIUKI Ngotho	86/03/05	86/03/17	Tax consultant, Eastern & Southern Africa Management Institute, Arusha, Tanzania; former Dean of Commerce, University of Nairobi
KIHORO Wanyiri	86/07/30	86/10/08	Lawyer and land economist; detained on political grounds for three weeks in 1981; former education and program officer at the Africa Centre, London, UK, 1984-6; Ll.B, London University
KURIA Gibson Kamau	87/02/26	87/03/06	Lawyer and law lecturer, University of Nairobi; Ll.B, University of Oxford, UK
MIANO Gacheche	86/04/24	86/07/03	Former law student, University of Nairobi
MKANGI Katama	86/05/08	86/07/21	Senior lecturer in sociology, University of Nairobi; Ph.D, University of Sussex, UK, 1972
NGANGA Mukaru	86/04/04	86/07/03	Former lecturer in history, University of Nairobi. Former prisoner of conscience 1982-4
ONYANGO Patrick Ouma	86/05/21	86/07/21	Teacher, graduate of University of Nairobi

Note: Raila Odinga has also been detained under the same regulations since 1983.

56

APPENDIX III
PEOPLE TRIED AND CONVICTED OF POLITICAL OFFENCES FROM 1986 TO JUNE 1987

Name	Arrest Date (Y/M/D)	Trial Date (Y/M/D)	Charge (see key below)	Prison Sentence	Personal Details
ACHIRA James Omwenga	86/12/15	87/01/29	E	2 years	journalist
ADONGO Justin Maurice Ogonyi	86/04/16	86/05/09	A	15 mths	lecturer
AGUTU Vitalis Owinyo	86/11/00	86/12/17	E	4 years	railways employee
ATIENO Ernest Owuor	87/02/09	87/03/06	E	4 years	clerk
ATITO Opanyi Mwai	87/02/00	87/03/09	E	4 years	businessman
AWITI Adhu	87/02/10	87/03/11	A	4 1/2 years	clerk
CHEGE Charles Wainaina	86/04/00	86/06/26	B	3 years	clerk
CHEGE Peter	86/12/00	87/01/23	E	5 years	businessman
IMBO Silas Awuor	87/03/00	87/04/03	E	4 years	clerk
KABASELLEH Ochieng	86/09/00	86/10/29	G	3 years	musician
KAHIRI James Mwangi	86/10/00	86/06/30	A	15 mths	teacher
KAHUHA Munyui	86/06/13	86/06/30	C	4 years	businessman
KAMANA Kimunya	86/12/00	87/02/03	E	4 years	KANU official
KAMANGARA John Maina	86/12/04	87/01/29	A	15 months	businessman/politician
KARANJA Francis Nduthu	86/12/30	87/01/23	A	5 years	farmer
KARANJA Joseph Gichuki	86/06/30	86/07/10	C	5 years	businessman
KARIUKI Benedict Munene	86/06/26	86/07/07	C	5 years	schoolteacher
KARIUKI Francis Chege	86/11/00	86/12/26	E	4 years	businessman
KIHARA Joshua Njoroge	86/06/30	86/07/10	B	5 years	schoolteacher
KIHARA Peter Gathoga	86/01/23	86/03/26	B	4 1/2 yrs	farmer
KIHARA Samuel Ndiba	86/03/00	86/06/11	A	fined	farmer
KIHORO Karige	86/07/28	86/08/07	A	18 mths	businessman
KIMONDO Kiruhi	86/07/00	86/08/00	A	fined	former councillor
KIRIAMITI John Baptista Wanjohi	87/01/20	87/02/12	E	7 years	writer
KITUR Philip Tirop arap	86/06/00	86/07/04	D	7 years	former law student
LUMUMBA Richard Odenda	86/04/00	86/04/25	C	4 years	schoolteacher
MAHUGU Michael Danson	87/02/00	87/03/16	E	4 years	businessman
MAINA Geoffrey Kiongo	86/03/05	86/03/25	B	5 years	accountant
MANJE Joseph Kamonye	86/03/12	86/03/25	B	5 years	lecturer
MATHENGE Remjioh Mwangi "Kaggia"	86/12/00	87/02/03	E	4 years	businessman
MBAJA Oyangi	86/03/05	86/03/26	A	2 1/2 yrs	businessman
MBURU Stanley Muchugia	86/05/00	86/07/08	C	5 years	bank messenger
MGHANGA Julius Mwandawiro	86/04/01	86/04/29	B	5 years	schoolteacher

Name					
MIANO Joseph Kariuru	86/12/30	87/01/23	E	4 years	municipal councillor
MOMANYI Peter Nyangau	87/02/00	87/04/14	F	15 months	former student
MUCHIRI Macharia	87/03/00	87/03/31	E	7 years	farmer
MUNGAI Samuel Kangethe	86/06/00	86/07/04	D	7 years	civil servant
MURATHE David Wakairu Gatuhi	86/12/00	87/02/05	A	15 mths	businessman
MUSAMALI Khauka Masaka	86/04/00	86/05/08	F	10 mths	schoolteacher
MUTAHI Joseph Njuguna	86/10/15	86/11/14	A	15 mths	journalist
MUTAHI Paul Wahome	86/10/15	86/11/14	A	15 mths	journalist
MUTHIGANI Wanderi	86/05/08	86/05/15	A	15 mths	law graduate
MUTHIKE Peter Kitusa	87/03/00	87/04/03	F	6 mths	factory worker
MUTONYA David Njuguna	86/04/29	86/05/09	B	4 years	civil servant
MUYELA Nelson Akhahukwa	86/12/00	87/01/02	C	3 years	railways employee
MWAI Justus Opany	87/02/09	87/03/09	E	4 years	businessman
MWAIRO David Chome	86/04/00	86/05/06	A	15 mths	post office employee
MWANGI Elijah Bernard	86/08/00	86/08/00	A	fined	librarian
MZIRAI David Kishushe Lengazi	86/04/16	86/05/05	B	4 1/2 yrs	civil servant
NDABI Elly John Gitau	86/04/00	86/06/25	C	7 years	businessman
NDERI Herman Marine	86/12/00	87/01/28	E	4 1/2 years	former police officer
NDINGO Peter Njuguna	86/03/28	86/04/04	B	4 years	engineering technician
NDUNGU Raphael Kariuki	87/01/00	87/02/12	A	15 months	former civil servant
NDUTHU Karimi	86/06/00	86/07/04	D	7 years	former engineering student
NDUTHU Francis Karimi	86/12/00	87/01/23	E	10 years	businessman
NJOROGE Charles Kangara	86/03/05	86/04/07	A	15 mths	businessman
NJOROGE George Mwaura	86/10/21	86/11/20	A	15 months	accountant
NYAKUNDI Fred Osoyo	87/02/00	87/04/16	F	15 months	former student
ODERA Daniel Tito	87/02/09	87/04/24	E	3 years	businessman
ODOTI Samuel Onyango	87/03/00	87/04/02	F	6 months	hotel employee
ODUOR Sylvanus Christopher Okech	86/09/24	86/12/09	E	6 years	assistant executive officer
OGONDA Charles	87/05/00	87/06/09	E	3 years	municipal employee
OJIJO Daniel Tom	87/02/00	87/04/24	E	3 years	businessman
OKECH Shem Ogola	86/10/00	86/11/14	E	3 years	bank employee
OLEL Odhiambo	87/03/20	87/04/06	E	5 years	doctor
ONDEWE Alex Okoth	86/10/19	86/11/21	E	4 years	businessman
ONGOMBE Odungi Randa	86/11/00	86/12/26	E	4 years	businessman
ONGWEN George Fanuel Oduor	86/04/00	86/04/29	C	4 years	schoolteacher
ONYANGO Cornels Akelo	86/04/02	86/05/05	B	4 years	civil servant
OPIATA James Odindo	86/03/27	86/04/10	B	4 years	postgraduate law student
OSEWE Walter Edward	86/11/00	86/12/01	B	4 years	former church employee
OSUNDWA George Chitechi	86/03/05	86/03/27	A	18 mths	former student
RUNGURWA Frederick Kariithi	86/06/18	86/06/26	B	3 years	unemployed
THIONGO John Gupta Nganga	86/05/08	86/05/15	A	15 mths	law graduate

Name			Charge	Sentence	Occupation
WAHEIRE Bernard Wachira	86/11/00	86/12/01	E	4 years	railways employee
WANDERI Mugo Theuri	86/09/22	86/11/07	E	4 years	journalist
WANDUI Naftali Karanja	86/06/00	86/07/07	C	4 1/2 yrs	schoolteacher
WANGUTHI Stephen Njoroge	86/06/12	86/06/26	C	6 years	civil servant
WANYOIKE David Njuguna	86/10/21	86/11/19	A	15 mths	mechanical engineer
WARUIRU John Mungai	86/06/00	86/06/23	C	7 years	carpenter
WEKESA Richard Nixon	87/02/00	87/04/06	F	10 years	former student

Key to charges (main charge only)
A "neglecting to report a felony"
B "possession of seditious publication(s)"
C "distribution of seditious publication(s)"
D "sabotage"
E "taking an unlawful oath"
F other charge, not involving use or advocacy of violence
G other charge, involving possible advocacy of violence

Note on dates: 00 indicates day of month not known

Information from Amnesty International

This paper is part of Amnesty International's publications program. As part of its effort to mobilize world public opinion in defence of the victims of human rights violations, Amnesty International produces a monthly Newsletter, an annual report, and reports, briefings and other documents on countries in all quarters of the globe.

Amnesty International attaches great importance to impartial and accurate reporting of facts. Its activities depend on meticulous research into allegations of human rights violations. The International Secretariat in London (with a staff of over 200, comprising some 40 nationalities)has a Research Department which collects and analyses information from a wide variety of sources. These include hundreds of newspapers and journals, government bulletins, transcriptions of radio broadcasts, reports from lawyers and humanitarian organizations, as well as letters from prisoners and their families. Amnesty International also sends fact-finding missions for on-the-spot investigations and to observe trials, meet prisoners and interview government officials. Amnesty International takes full responsibility for its published reports and if proved wrong on any point is prepared to issue a correction.

How to subscribe to Amnesty International

A subscription to Amnesty International will give you access to information about human rights abuses produced on a global, independent and impartial basis. You will also receive details on how you can help the people who are the victims.

Amnesty International Newsletter

This monthly bulletin is a regular update on Amnesty International's work: reports of fact-finding missions, details of political prisoners, reliable reports of torture and executions. It is written—without political bias—for human rights activists throughout the world and is widely used by journalists, students, political leaders, doctors, lawyers and other professionals.

Amnesty International Report

This annual report is a country-by-country survey of Amnesty International's work to combat political imprisonment, torture and the death penalty throughout the world. In describing the organization's work, the report provides details of human rights abuses in over 120 countries. It is probably the most widely read—and most influential—of the many reports published by Amnesty International each year.

- ✂ - - - - -

ease detach this form and return to the Amnesty International section in your country or to: Amnesty International Publications, Easton Street, London WC1X 8DJ, United Kingdom.

I wish to subscribe to the *Amnesty International Newsletter* (1987 prices: £5.00, US$12.50).
I wish to subscribe to the monthly *Amnesty International Newsletter* and yearly *Amnesty International Report* (1987 prices: £15.00, US$37.50).
Please send me further details of Amnesty International Publications.

ame_____ Address _____

_____

_____

KENYA: TORTURE, POLITICAL DETENTION AND UNFAIR TRIALS

Human rights have come under serious attack in Kenya in the past year as the government appears to have adopted a deliberate program to silence or intimidate its political opponents. Prisoners of conscience have been tortured and detained indefinitely by administrative order. Other political prisoners have been secretly and illegally detained, tortured into making false confessions and then jailed for years after unfair trials.

Most victims of human rights abuse have been arrested on suspicion of having links with a clandestine opposition group but many appear to have done no more than criticize the way the country is run.

At least two political prisoners have died in custody. The body of one was found to be bruised, wounded and emaciated with skin blistering and peeling off — just 21 days after he had been seized by Kenyan Special Branch officers.

Similar effects have been reported after the "swimming pool" torture used by the Special Branch, in which prisoners have been held naked for long periods in waterlogged underground cells, in some cases until their feet began to rot. Other tortures have included starvation and brutal beatings with truncheons, chair legs and lengths of rubber hose. Complaints about torture and prolonged "disappearance" of prisoners during interrogation have been ignored or dismissed by the courts.

In this new report the worldwide human rights organization Amnesty International says the government crackdown began in March 1986 and that since then senior government and law officers appear to have condoned the undermining of crucial legal and constitutional safeguards, resulting in a serious abuse of the rule of law in Kenya.